Table of Contents

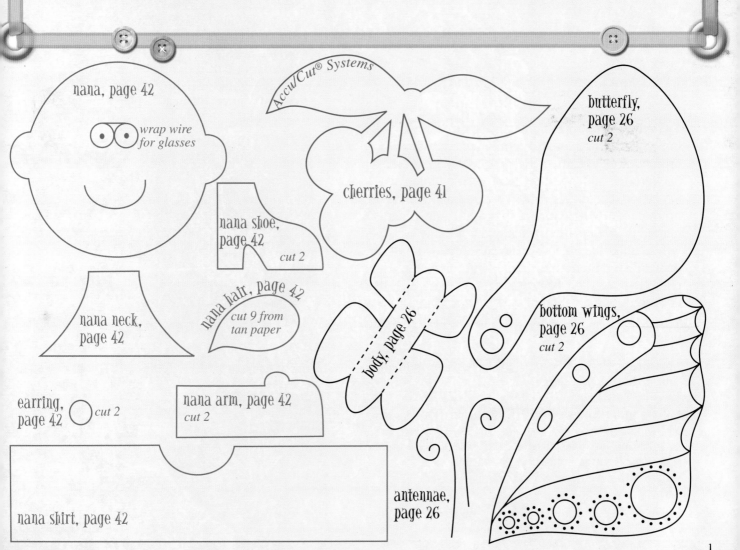

nana, page 42

wrap wire for glasses

AccuCut® Systems

cherries, page 41

butterfly, page 26
cut 2

nana shoe, page 42
cut 2

nana neck, page 42

nana hair, page 42
cut 9 from tan paper

body, page 26

bottom wings, page 26
cut 2

earring, page 42 *cut 2*

nana arm, page 42
cut 2

antennae, page 26

nana shirt, page 42

Beads

All Things Bright and Beautiful

dragonfly wings

place on fold

Shauna created a fabulous theme with beads, collage and vellum papers. She matted each photo on silver. The close-up photo was matted onto torn rectangles of mesh vellum, then purple vellum. She used purple chalk to highlight the mesh edges, then fastened the photo mat to a lavender collage background with a silver eyelet in each corner. Shauna used the dragonfly on the background to create a 3-dimensional version with the beads and mesh vellum. The wings were outlined with the silver pen.

- **specialty Paper Pizazz™:** pastel purple vellum (*12"x12" Pastel Vellum Papers,* also by the sheet); mesh vellum (*Lacy Vellum*); silver (*Metallic Silver,* also by the sheet)
- **patterned Paper Pizazz™:** lavender collage with dragonflies (*Soft Collage Papers*)
- **purple, turquoise, white beads:** Blue Moon Beads/Elizabeth Ward & Co., Inc.
- **photography:** Yuen Lui
- **4 silver eyelets:** Stamp Studio
- **silver beading filament:** Kreinik Metallics
- **purple decorating chalks:** Craf-T Products
- **24-gauge violet wire:** Artistic Wire, Ltd.™
- **pop up glue dots:** Glue Dots, Inc.
- **purple pen:** Sakura Gelly Roll
- **silver pen:** Pentel Hybrid Gel Roller
- **voluta computer font:** Creating Keepsakes
- **page designer:** Shauna Berglund-Immel

Twinkling Christmas lights turned on Shauna's imagination for a creative holiday theme set with bright colored beads. She began with a green mesh background and cut along the patterned lines of a 5" wide rectangle of green pinking paper and brightened it with a torn strip of blue dots. Shauna matted the letters onto white and randomly wrapped wire around the letters with beads threaded on top; then adhered them to the page with foam tape. Her photo is matted on white, blue mesh and white; then anchored with a strand of beads along the bottom edge to balance the page. The photo was placed on the page with foam tape.

- **patterned Paper Pizazz™:** green mesh, green pinking, blue mesh, blue dots (*Jewel Tints*)
- **solid Paper Pizazz™:** white (*Plain Pastels*)
- **36 Summer Splash matte beads:** Blue Moon Beads/ Elizabeth Ward & Co., Inc.
- **2" school house letters die-cuts:** Accu/Cut® Systems
- **36" of 24-gauge gold wire:** Artistic Wire Ltd.™
- **foam adhesive tape:** Scotch® Brand
- **white pen:** Pental Milky Gel Roller
- **page designer:** Shauna Berglund-Immel

Shauna captured the magic and sparkle of romance in this lovely page. She used lavender sponged paper for a background, then tore the right edges of pink vellum and of stripes for a border. She matted her photo on pink vellum and lavender flowers with torn edges; then thread alternating colors of beads onto gold thread to frame her photo. She wrote "loves" with the glue pen, then placed another strand of beads on top. The heart dangles from a pretty bow secured with a glue dot in the upper right corner.

- **specialty Paper Pizazz™:** pastel pink vellum (*12"x12" Pastel Vellum Papers*, also by the sheet)
- **patterned Paper Pizazz™:** lavender/pink stripes with dragonflies, lavender flowers, lavender sponged (*Mixing Light Papers*)
- **purple, pink seed beads:** Blue Moon Beads/ Elizabeth Ward & Co., Inc.
- **⅝" wide gold heart locket:** Creative Beginnings
- **8" of ⅝" wide pink sheer ribbon:** Sheer Creations
- **metallic gold thread:** Wrights®
- **glitter:** Rubber Stampede Glitter Sparkles
- **glue pen:** Mounting Memories Keepsake Glue™
- **glue dots:** Glue Dots™ International LLC
- **penman, script, cursive, calligraphy, toggle computer fonts:** Creating Keepsakes
- **page designer:** Shauna Berglund-Immel

Travis and Trea
from High School Sweethearts to Man and Wife

I have found the one whom my soul loves
Song of Solomon 3:4

2001

Shauna chose exotic beads for this trophy page. The giraffe provided the inspiration for her border. She tore her shapes from the patterned papers and vellums, then used decorating chalks to enhance the edges. Each photo was matted on gold and a beige textured paper with torn edges. She used the punch to make five holes along the bottom of the tag, threaded one of each bead onto a strand of gold thread and secured each onto the tag. She combined raffia, copper thread and gold cord and knotted it through the tag hole.

- **specialty Paper Pizazz™:** tan vellum, ivory vellum (*12"x12" Pastel Vellum Papers*, also by the sheet); gold (*Metallic Gold*, also by the sheet)
- **patterned Paper Pizazz™:** beige scales, beige spattered, beige speckled (*Soft & Subtle Textures*); 12"x12" sandstone (by the sheet)
- **dark brown, light brown, black decorating chalks:** Craf-T Products
- **5 tan tube, 5 black flat, 5 black twist beads:** Blue Moon Beads/Elizabeth Ward & Co., Inc.
- **18" metallic gold thread:** Wrights®
- **14" metallic gold stretch cord**
- **14" copper embroidery thread:** DMC
- **7" of raffia**
- **1⅝"x3¼" ivory tag:** Paper Reflections
- **1/16" hole punch:** McGill, Inc.
- **brown, black pens:** Zig® Writer
- **page designer:** Shauna Berglund-Immel

Wildlife Safari May 2001

Beads

Shauna captured this golden moment with gold beads for a stunning effect. She chose gold stripes and gold leaves for a layered background, separated with a ⅛" strip of gold. She matted the photo on tan vellum, leaving a ½" border and used a punch on each corner. She outlined the vellum edges in gold and wrapped gold thread around each corner, strung with beads along the top and bottom. The tags were cut from brown sponged paper, covered with tan vellum and outlined in gold. She glued the materials to each tag as shown, attached an eyelet at the top of each and affixed them to the page with foam tape. She cut the ribbon in thirds, knotted each at the center and glued one above each tag. She completed the page by wrapping gold thread through each eyelet to the ribbon above and knotting the ends to secure.

- **specialty Paper Pizazz™:** pastel tan vellum (*12"x12" Pastel Vellum Papers*, also by the sheet)
- **patterned Paper Pizazz™:** brown/gold stripes, brown/gold leaves (*Metallic Gold*); gold (*Metallic Gold,* also by the sheet); brown sponged with gold splatters (*Spattered, Crackled & Sponged*)
- **20 gold beads:** Westrim® Crafts
- **3 gold eyelets:** Stamp Studio
- **3 beige/brown buttons**
- **1½"x3" tag die-cut:** Accu/Cut® Systems
- **4 silver eyelets, corner punch:** Stamp Studio
- **metallic gold thread:** Wrights®
- **15" of ⅝" wide white sheer ribbon with gold edges:** C.M. Offray & Son, Inc.
- **3 gold skeleton leaves:** Black Ink
- **3 pieces of brown sea glass**
- **gold pen:** Pentel Hybrid Gel Roller
- **black pen:** Sakura Gelly Roll
- **glue dots:** Glue Dots™ International LLC
- **foam adhesive tape:** Scotch® Brand
- **page designer:** Shauna Berglund-Immel

Shauna chose subtle bead accents to highlight this captivating photo. She sewed the seed beads in a cluster at the center of the daisy on the collage paper for a striking effect. She placed a 5¼"x12" rectangle of white vellum on the left side of the page; then secured it to the page by sewing a sead bead to each corner and knotting the thread at the back. She matted the photo on blue lavender vellum, leaving a ⅛" border. The blue pen was used for journaling.

- **specialty Paper Pizazz™:** blue lavender vellum (12"x12" *Pastel Vellum Papers*); white vellum (by the sheet)
- **patterned Paper Pizazz™:** purple daisy collage (*Soft Collage Papers*)
- **sapphire luster seed beads:** Blue Moon Beads/ Elizabeth Ward & Co., Inc.
- **metallic gold thread:** Wrights®
- **sewing needle**
- **blue pen:** Sakura Gelly Roll
- **bella computer font:** Creating Keepsakes
- **page designer:** Shauna Berglund-Immel

Shauna spelled out her favorite Valentine in alphabet beads! She used pink tiles with words as a background paper, then matted the white words on pink paper onto white and used the scallop scissors. Shauna matted Kaelin's photo on white, then yellow, leaving ½" border along the bottom edge. She strung alphabet beads onto ribbon and inserted the ends into an eyelet at each lower corner. She matted the photo on white, trimmed the edges and outlined the scallops with the salmon pen. Shauna used the white pen to journal on a torn rectangle of white vellum. She used the wide ribbon to tie a shoestring bow and glued it above the photo. She punched three flowers from yellow and inserted an eyelet in each center. Glue dots were used to attach the flowers to the page.

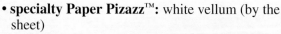

- **specialty Paper Pizazz™:** white vellum (by the sheet)
- **patterned Paper Pizazz™:** white words on pink, pink tiles with words (*Mixing Light Papers*)
- **solid Paper Pizazz™:** yellow (*Solid Muted Colors*); white (*Plain Pastels*)
- **alpha beads:** Darice, Inc.
- **5 pink eyelets:** Stamp Studio
- **6" of ¹⁄₁₆", 12" of ⅝" wide white satin ribbon:** C.M. Offray & Son, Inc.
- **1" wide flower punch:** Marvy® Uchida
- **mini-scallop, scallop decorative scissors:** Fiskars®
- **salmon pen:** Zig® Writer
- **white pen:** Pentel Milky Gel Roller
- **glue dots:** Glue Dots™ International LLC
- **page designer:** Shauna Berglund-Immel

LeNae added glistening beads to embellish her winter wonderland page. She began with lines/dots on navy for a background, then glued an 8½"x11½" rectangle of snowflakes on burgundy, matted on white to the right side of the page. She embellished the snowflake cut-outs with seed beads, then glued them to the page as shown. She matted two photos each on white, used scallop scissors to trim the edges, then matted each on navy. She journaled on white and glued it to a rectangle of snowflakes on blue, then matted it on white and trimmed the edges with the scallop scissors.

- **patterned Paper Pizazz™:** snowflakes on navy, snowflakes on burgundy, lines/dots on navy (*Mixing Christmas Papers*)
- **solid Paper Pizazz™:** navy (*Solid Jewel Tones*); white (*12"x12" Solid Pastel Papers*)
- **snowman, snowflake motifs:** (*Paper Pizazz™ Annie Lang's Big Cut-Outs™*)
- **white seed beads:** Blue Moon Beads/Elizabeth Ward & Co., Inc.
- **mini-pinking decorative scissors:** Fiskars®
- **black pen:** Zig® Millennium
- **glue pen:** Mounting Memories Keepsake Glue™
- **page designer:** LeNae Gerig

Buttons

Shauna matched a precious photo with pretty papers and buttoned it all together for a fabulous look! She matted a 10¾"x11⅛" rectangle of yellow with stars & buttons on white and centered it on a blue/pink checks background. She cut a heart from pink. She cut a column from the blue with stars & buttons paper and used thread to sew the buttons. The heart and column were matted on white, trimmed with the decorative scissors and glued to the page as shown. The photo is matted on white, yellow, then on pink with chalked edges. The photo mat was then glued to a 6½"x9¼" rectangle of white, matted on blue and glued it to the page. Thread was threaded through each button and glued to the page. She punched stars from yellow and blue, chalked and glued them to the photo mat, and journaled as shown.

- **patterned Paper Pizazz™:** blue/pink checks, yellow with small stars & buttons, blue with stars & buttons (*Mixing Bright Papers*)
- **solid Paper Pizazz™:** pink, blue, yellow, white (*12"x12" Solid Plain Pastels*)
- **¹³⁄₁₆" wide pink gingham, blue gingham, yellow gingham buttons:** Dress It Up, Change Your Buttons
- **⁷⁄₁₆" wide blue, ⁹⁄₁₆" wide red buttons**
- **black decorating chalk:** Craf-T Products
- **⅝" wide star punch:** Marvy® Uchida
- **3" wide heart die-cut:** Accu/Cut® Systems
- **white embroidery thread:** DMC
- **mini-scallop decorative scissors:** Fiskars®
- **glue dots:** Glue Dots™ International LLC
- **foam adhesive tape:** Scotch® Brand
- **black pen:** Zig® Writer
- **handprint computer font:** Creating Keepsakes
- **page designer:** Shauna Berglund-Immel

A rose can inspire the heart, as Shauna shows here. She started with a rectangle of black with pink dots; matted it on white and trimmed the edges with the decorative scissors and glued on a black background. The photo and hearts were matted on black and white. Eyelets and ribbon were attached to each heart and wrapped around each button as shown. The sheer ribbon was tied in a shoestring bow and glued above the photo.

- **patterned Paper Pizazz™:** black with pink dots/pink swirls, pink/burgundy stripes, pink paisley (*Jewel Tints*)
- **solid Paper Pizazz™:** black (*Solid Jewel Tones*); white (*Plain Pastels*)
- **three ⅝" wide white buttons**
- **six white eyelets:** Stamp Studio
- **black embroidery thread:** DMC
- **20" of ⅛" wide black satin ribbon:** C.M. Offray & Son, Inc.
- **10" of ⅝" wide pink sheer ribbon:** Sheer Creations
- **mini-scallop decorative scissors:** Fiskars®
- **2⅜" wide heart punch:** Marvy® Uchida
- **foam adhesive tape:** Scotch® Brand
- **page designer:** Shauna Berglund-Immel

Lisa created a whimsical theme with bee buttons and patterned papers. She cut a 12"x6" rectangle of grass paper and trimmed the top edge with deckle scissors. She cut a 7¾"x7" rectangle of plaid, trimmed the edges and wrapped it over the top of the grass; then glued it to the bottom of the clouds paper. She journaled on white, then matted it and her photo on red and white. She cut out the hotdog and attached it and the ant buttons with foam tape. A bee button is affixed to each side of the photo, with looped lines drawn with the black pen.

- **patterned Paper Pizazz™:** 12"x12" clouds, 12"x12" grass, picnic ants, Christmas plaid (by the sheet)
- **solid Paper Pizazz™:** red (*Solid Jewel Tones*); white (*Solid Pastel Papers*)
- **2 bee, 10 ant buttons:** Jesse James Button and Trim
- **deckle, pinking decorative scossors:** Fiskars®
- **foam adhesive tape:** Scotch® Brand
- **black pen:** Sakura 3mm Micron
- **page designer:** Lisa Garcia-Bergstedt

Our Annual May Day Picnic

May 1, 2001

When Jon and I met our first date was actually on May 1st. On our date we had a picnic. In Volunteer Park. So as a tradition we have a picnic every May 1st. No matter what day that it falls on. Rain or shine. This has been a tradition for the past 9 years. We have so many stories of our picnics together. There have been good ones and there have been bad ones. But we make it a point to muster up the moral to go every year. There has been rain, and yes there has been ants. But each one is special and I look forward, always, to the next year.

Ivy Peterson
May 1959

Arlene created a lovely theme with filigree heart buttons to frame her great-grandmother's photo. She cut a 9¼"x9¾" rectangle from the small flowers paper, matted it on purple vellum, scuffed plum paper, then white vellum, each with a ¼" mat. Her photo is matted on purple, then white vellums. She cut two 1¼"x8⅞" rectangles of blue/purple lines and matted each on purple and white vellums. She inserted purple embroidery thread through the four green buttons and green thread through six purple buttons and glued the ends to the back of the blue/purple lines mats. The remaining two green buttons were glued at each end of a 4½"x1¼" purple vellum rectangle, matted on white vellum.

- **specialty Paper Pizazz™:** pastel purple vellum, white vellum (by the sheet)
- **patterned Paper Pizazz™:** flowers on navy, small flowers on navy, scuffed plum, blue/purple lines (*Mixing Heritage Papers*)
- **6 plum, 6 green ⅜" wide filigree heart buttons:** Dress It Up
- **pearlescent lavender, green embroidery thread:** DMC
- **page designer:** Arlene Peterson

Charms

Lisa chose garden motif charms to add the perfect touch to her floral theme. She began with a background of black dots on purple, then cut along the petals of the pansies paper, matted on goldenrod and glued to the bottom edge. She cut four purple 1" squares and matted each on goldenrod. Lisa used purple thread to sew each charm to a square, then used foam tape to attach each to a 2" black square, matted on goldenrod. Her photo is matted on purple, goldenrod, then black. She double journaled on a 10⅛"x¾" strip of white vellum. Two pansies were cut out and attached to the strip with foam tape.

- **specialty Paper Pizazz™:** white vellum (by the sheet)
- **patterned Paper Pizazz™:** 12"x12" black dots on purple, 12"x12" pansies (by the sheet)
- **solid Paper Pizazz™:** goldenrod (*Solid Bright Papers*); black, purple (*Solid Jewel Tones*)
- **flowerpot, wheelbarrow, watering can, seed packet charms:** S. Axelrod Company
- **metallic purple thread:** DMC
- **sewing needle**
- **foam adhesive tape:** Scotch® Brand
- **black pen:** Sakura 5mm Micron
- **page designer:** Lisa Garcia-Bergstedt

LeNae created a lovely theme for her heritage photo with charms, lace and collage paper. She matted her photo on ivory, then cut the gold thread in 1"-2½" lengths to hang six charms, taping the top ends to the bottom of the photo back. She matted the photo on pink rose paper, then again on ivory. She glued lace ribbon along the top and bottom edge of the photo. She journaled on a rectangle of ivory, then used ½"-1" lengths of gold thread to hang the remaining charms along the top edge. She matted it in on burgundy, pink rose, then ivory and glued lace ribbon along the top edge.

- **patterned Paper Pizazz™:** white rose collage (*Holidays & Seasons Collage Papers*); pink rose (*Pretty Collage Papers,* also by the sheet)
- **solid Paper Pizazz™:** ivory (*Plain Pastels*); burgundy (*Solid Jewel Tones*)
- **11 heart lockets and charms:** S. Axelrod Company
- **metallic gold thread:** Wrights®
- **12" of ⅝" wide floral lace ribbon:** C.M. Offray & Son, Inc.
- **glue dots:** Glue Dots™ International LLC
- **page designer:** LeNae Gerig

LeNae and Lisa teamed up to make a perfect friendship page with charms, fibers and a vellum pocket. A 1"-1½" gap was torn near the left side of the blue/purple lines paper, then eyelets were inserted on each side and fibers threaded through the eyelets. A strip of purple scuffed paper was glued behind the laced gap. Each photo was matted on purple scuffed, then the edges were torn, a set of holes were punched into each corner and fibers were tied through each corner. The vellum pocket was matted on torn strips of purple, blue, pink and white vellums. The charms were strung onto embroidery thread as shown. The black pen was used to journal on pink vellum, with the edges torn and fiber wrapped through a set of holes at each end.

- **specialty Paper Pizazz™:** pastel pink vellum, pastel purple vellum, pastel blue vellum (*12"x12" Pastel Vellum Papers*, also by the sheet); white vellum (by the sheet)
- **patterned Paper Pizazz™:** purple scuffed, blue/purple lines (*Mixing Heritage Papers*)
- **sunshine pocket:** *Paper Pizazz™ Vellum Envelopes & Pockets Cut-Outs™*
- **star, moon charms:** Creative Beginnings
- **purple, gold fibers:** Adornaments™
- **ten gold eyelets:** Stamp Studio
- **⅛" wide circle punch:** Marvy® Uchida
- **black emroidery thread:** DMC
- **black pen:** Zig® Millennium
- **mini glue dots:** Glue Dots™ International LLC
- **page designer:** LeNae Gerig & Lisa Garcia-Bergstedt

Susan preserved an heirloom photo in exquisite detail with charms and patterned vellums. She layered tan vines vellum onto yellow stripes paper, then placed a 7¼"x9½" rectangle of tan vellum along the right edge with photo corners. She glued an 8½"x½" strip of tan vellum onto an 8½"x2" strip of tan stripes and glued it to the page center. She matted her heirloom photo on ivory and tan vellum, used the corner punch and outlined the edges with the gold pen. For the charm pockets, Susan cut three 2½" squares of filigree on stripes vellum, folded each corner inward to meet in the center, then folded each corner ½" outward. Each charm was secured with a glue dot. Susan threaded beads and a heart charm onto wire, wrapped it around a vellum pocket and inserted a ivory rectangle inside.

- **specialty Paper Pizazz™:** yellow stripes (*Soft Tints*)
- **patterned Paper Pizazz™:** tan vines vellum, tan filigree vellum, tan stripes vellum (*Tone-on-Tone Vellum*); pastel tan vellum, ivory vellum (*12"x12" Pastel Vellum Papers*, also by the sheet)
- **solid Paper Pizazz™:** ivory (*Plain Pastels*)
- **charms:** S. Axelrod Company
- **4 frosted violet glass beads, 50 tan seed beads:** Blue Moon Beads/Elizabeth Ward & Co., Inc.
- **metallic gold thread, 32-gauge gold wire:** Westrim® Crafts
- **4 gold photo corners:** Canson-Talens, Inc.
- **corner punch:** McGill
- **gold pen:** Pentel Hybrid Gel Roller
- **mini glue dots:** Glue Dots™ International LLC
- **page designer:** Susan Cobb

Coins

Shauna discovered a wealth of possibilities using coins in this page. To tie her theme together, the treasure chest collage was perfect. She matted her family portrait on gold and torn rectangles of peach and ivory vellums, chalking the edges for a rustic effect. She tore a 9" long strip each of tan and ivory vellum, chalked the edges and placed them with the matted photo on the page with eyelets as shown. Shauna tucked coins randomly inside the layers, securing them with glue dots. She used the gold pen to highlight the details on the chest and the black pen for journaling. It's a treasure!

- **specialty Paper Pizazz™:** tan vellum, ivory vellum, pastel peach vellum (*12"x12" Pastel Vellum Papers*, also by the sheet); gold (*Metallic Gold Papers*, also by the sheet)
- **patterned Paper Pizazz™:** treasure chest collage (*Masculine Collage Papers*)
- **dark brown, medium brown, light brown decorating chalks:** Craf-T Products
- **⅛" wide gold & silver, ³⁄₁₆" wide gold eyelets:** Stamp Studio
- **glue dots:** Glue Dots™ International LLC
- **gold, black pens:** Sakura Gelly Roll
- **page designer:** Shauna Berglund-Immel

Shauna created a stunning silver theme to preserve quarters from the Tooth Fairy. She matted two photos each on silver, then together on black. She inserted three washers and fasteners along the top and bottom edges of the mat. She cut three 1¾" squares each from white vellum and white tri-dots on black paper. With the vellum on top, she sewed silver thread around the side and bottom edges. She cut seven teeth and three tooth fairy motifs from the patterned paper, inserting one tooth and coin into each pocket with fairies glued to the pockets as shown. She glued a 3" length of thread to connect each pocket with a fastener on the black mat. She journaled with the silver and black pens and tied a knot in the ribbon before gluing as shown.

- **specialty Paper Pizazz™:** black/silver stripes (*Metallic Silver*); silver (*Metallic Silver*, also by the sheet); white vellum (by the sheet)
- **patterned Paper Pizazz™:** white tri-dots on black (*Heritage Papers*); tooth fairy (*Childhood Memories*)
- **solid Paper Pizazz™:** black (*Solid Jewel Tones*)
- **silver thread, sewing needle:** Wrights®
- **6" of ½" wide black satin ribbon:** C.M. Offray & Son, Inc.
- **six ⅛" wide silver fasteners & washers:** Hyglo/ AmericanPin
- **glue dots:** Glue Dots™ International LLC
- **silver pen:** Pentel Hybrid Gel Roller
- **black pen:** Sakura Gelly Roll
- **page designer:** Shauna Berglund-Immel

Shauna preserved a little piece of history with this sophisticated Southwestern theme and special coins. She cut the following vellums: 2"x12" of ivory, 3½"x12" of peach and a 5"x12" of blue vellum. She tore along the right edge of each, chalked the torn edges, then layered the vellums along the left side of the Southwest symbols collage paper. She inserted an eyelet along the top and bottom of each layer. Shauna matted the Southwest collage tags on gold, inserted one eyelet in each round tag and three on the bottom of the large tag. The large eyelet was inserted at the top of the large tag, with the fibers tied around it. Shauna used two 3" lengths of thin fiber strands to attach the two circle tags to the large tag. She matted Spencer's photo on gold. Shauna glued Spencer's two special coins in the bottom corner. She used the black pen for journaling on the vellum layers and page.

- **specialty Paper Pizazz™**: pastel blue vellum, pastel peach vellum (*12"x12" Pastel Vellum Papers*, also by the sheet); ivory vellum (by the sheet); gold (*Metallic Gold*, also by the sheet)
- **patterned Paper Pizazz™**: Southwest symbols collage (*Vacation Collage*)
- **tags**: *Paper Pizazz™ Tag Art Cut-Outs™*
- **eleven ⅛" wide, one ¼" wide gold eyelets**: Stamp Studio
- **multiple red/orange fibers**: Adornaments™
- **black decorating chalk**: Craf-T Products
- **foam adhesive tape**: Scotch® Brand
- **black pen**: Sakura Gelly Roll
- **page designer**: Shauna Berglund-Immel

Lisa created a bright new look for her piggybank complete with special coins. She began with pink stripes for a background. She matted her photo on white, then pink dots and another layer of white. She used the ribbon to make a shoestring bow and glued it to the bottom of the photo mat. She transferred the piggybank pattern onto pink vellum, cut it out and outlined the edges with the pink pen. She glued two coins to the back of the piggybank and one halfway in the top slot. She computer journaled on white, matted it on pink dots and white. She used the black pen to journal on the striped paper and vellum pig.

- **specialty Paper Pizazz™**: pastel pink vellum (*12"x12" Pastel Vellum Papers*, also by the sheet)
- **patterned Paper Pizazz™**: pink zig-zag stripes, pink dots (*12"x12" Bright Tints*)
- **solid Paper Pizazz™**: white (*Plain Pastels*)
- **9" of ¼" wide dark pink satin ribbon**: C.M. Offray & Son, Inc.
- **pink, black pens**: Sakura Gelly Roll
- **page designer**: Lisa Garcia-Bergstedt

Eyelets

Eyelets are wonderful additions to scrapbooking. Susan used silver eyelets for this elegant page. She began with green/silver leaves for a background. She cut a 6"x11" rectangle from green vellum, outlined it with the silver pen and centered it on the page with an eyelet attached to each corner. She cut 12"x4" and 3"x2" rectangles of white vellum, outlined each in silver, and placed them on the page with eyelets as shown. She matted the photos on silver. For the mini album, Susan cut three 4⅝"x5¾" rectangles each from green/silver stripes and silver papers and glued the backs of each stripes rectangle to the back of a silver piece. With the striped sides stacked facing up, she inserted three eyelets along the left edge and used wire to connect the layers, curling the ends to secure. Matted photos and journal boxes were glued to the inside pages. Susan used the silver pen to journal and add a vine motif on the vellums. She tied the ribbon in a shoestring bow.

- **specialty Paper Pizazz™**: green/silver stripes, green/silver leaves (*Metallic Silver*); 2 sheets of silver (*Metallic Silver*, also by the sheet); pastel green vellum (*12"x12" Pastel Vellum Papers*, also by the sheet); white vellum (by the sheet)
- **18 silver eyelets:** Stamp Studio
- **10" of ¼" wide white sheer ribbon:** C.M. Offray & Son, Inc.
- **24-gauge silver wire:** Artistic Wire, Ltd.™
- **⅛" wide hole punch:** Marvy® Uchida
- **wire cutters, pliers**
- **silver pen:** Sakura Gelly Roll
- **page designer:** Susan Cobb

Arlene created a magical page with eyelets and stars. She used the blue spattered with stars as a background. She cut 6⅝"x2½", 6⅝"x5½" and 12"x 2⅝" rectangles of pale yellow, with a torn rectangle of blue spattered paper for each yellow rectangle and glued to the page as shown. The photo was matted on yellow. Arlene used the small die-cut to make yellow vellum stars for the name and the large die-cut to make three each in yellow and blue vellums. She cut 3¾"x12" rectangles each of pale yellow and blue spattered, with the right edge of the spattered torn as shown. The large stars were attached to the mat with eyelets. Wire was used to form stars and attached to a vellum star with thread.

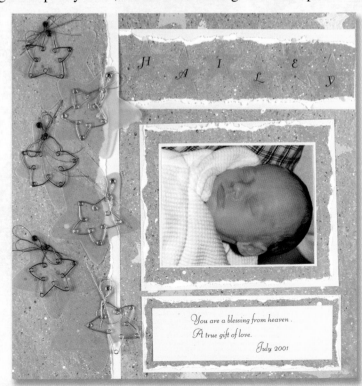

- **specialty Paper Pizazz™**: pastel blue vellum, pastel yellow vellum (*12"x12" Pastel Vellum Papers*, also by the sheet)
- **patterned Paper Pizazz™**: blue spattered, blue spattered with yellow stars (*Spattered, Crackled & Sponged*)
- **solid Paper Pizazz™:** pale yellow (*Plain Pastels*)
- **3 blue, 3 gold eyelets:** Stamp Studio
- **metallic gold, blue embroidery thread:** DMC
- **metallic blue, gold 24-gauge wire:** Artistic Wire, Ltd.™
- **mini star and star #2 die cuts:** Accu/Cut® Systems
- **page designer:** Arlene Peterson

Eyelets were the perfect addition to highlight the ladybug theme on this delightful page. Arlene began with a ladybugs background paper. She tore a 9¾"x10" rectangle of red scuffed paper, glued it to black and attached it to the page with an eyelet in each corner. She cut two 2"x12" strips from the bees on green paper, glued the ends together, then folded the top down ½", back an ⅛" and repeated to make a 9" long accordian. She glued it to black, placed a torn-edge ¾"x9" vellum strip in the center and attached an eyelet at the top and bottom. She inserted red cord from the back to the front and wrapped it around the vellum strip, inserting the end through the top eyelet. Two more eyelets were attached near the center to secure. Arlene matted Hailey's photo on bees on green, then black and tore out a vellum frame, wrapping it with the cord with eyelets in the corners. She journaled on vellum, matted it on bees on green and black, then glued a ladybug at each end and on the vellum strips.

- **specialty Paper Pizazz™:** white vellum (by the sheet)
- **patterned Paper Pizazz™:** bees on green, ladybugs on yellow checks, red scuffed (*Mixing Bright Papers*)
- **solid black paper**
- **14 black eyelets:** Stamp Studio
- **2 yards of metallic red cord:** C.M. Offray & Son, Inc.
- **page designer:** Arlene Peterson

Eyelets fit into any theme—even a nature scene as Arlene created here. She began with a green crackled background, with a 12"x7" rectangle of ivory vellum, torn along the long edges, affixed to the page top with an eyelet in each corner. Arlene wrapped gold thread around the vellum as shown. She matted two photos of the same size on black and ivory then glued them to the sides as shown. A vertical photo is matted on black and ivory, with the long sides even and glued to the center. Arlene die-cut the leaves, outlined them in gold pen and attached them to the page with eyelets. She tore a rectangle from ivory vellum for her journaling and attached it with eyelets. Gold thread connected the small leaves through the eyelets.

- **specialty Paper Pizazz™:** ivory vellum (*12"x12" Pastel Vellum Papers*, also by the sheet)
- **patterned Paper Pizazz™:** green crackled (*Spattered, Crackled & Sponged*)
- **solid Paper Pizazz™:** black (*Solid Jewel Tones*); ivory (*Plain Pastels*)
- **16 gold eyelets:** Stamp Studio
- **oak leaf, mini leaf die-cuts:** Accu/Cut® Systems
- **metallic gold embroidery thread:** DMC
- **foam adhesive tape:** Scotch® Brand
- **gold pen:** Pentel Hybrid Gel Roller
- **page designer:** Arlene Peterson

Eyelets

Lisa sailed the seven seas to find just the right eyelets for this fun page. She used blue ticking paper for a background, then tore the top edge from the swirls paper to resemble waves. She inserted two eyelets at each end. She cut 20" wire lengths, formed ½" tall loops and inserted the ends into the eyelets. She transferred the sail patterns (see page 48) onto vellum swirls, and yellow vellum then the hull onto crackle paper, matting the crackle on blue. She cut a ¼"x7" strip from barnwood and used foam tape to add height. Eyelets were inserted along the inside of each sail, with one more at the lower outside corners. Hemp was threaded through the eyelets and knotted at the end. Lisa matted her photo on white, blue then white again and attached it to the page with an eyelet in each corner.

- **specialty Paper Pizazz™:** pastel yellow vellum (*12"x12" Pastel Vellum Papers*, also by the sheet); vellum swirls (by the sheet)
- **patterned Paper Pizazz™:** bright tints blue swirls, bright tints blue ticking (*12"x12" Bright Tints*, also by the sheet); crackle, barnwood (by the sheet)
- **solid Paper Pizazz™:** white, blue (*Solid Pastel Papers*)
- **19 blue eyelets:** Stamp Studio
- **16" of hemp:** Westrim® Crafts
- **22-gauge blue wire:** Artistic Wire, Ltd.™
- **black pen:** Zig® Writer
- **foam adhesive tape:** Scotch® Brand
- **tracing paper, transfer paper**
- **page designer:** Lisa Garcia-Bergstedt

Lisa picked the perfect eyelets to adorn this delightful page. She used green gingham for a background. She cut 4" squares of purple checks, lavender dots and burgundy dots, each matted on a solid jewel tone paper, and attached them along the bottom edge with eyelets as shown. She used the patterns for the rabbit ears, egg and flower pot and punched the flowers as shown. She matted the egg on ivory, inserted eyelets randomly on the egg and attached it to the lower right square with foam tape. She matted her photos on green and attached the two smaller mats to the top left of the page. She cut three 9" lengths of wire, bent each slightly and attached them to the back of her large photo, then attached it to the page with foam tape. She inserted the large ears as shown, folding one over to meet the photo edge.

- **patterned Paper Pizazz™:** green gingham, purple checks, lavender dots, burgundy dots (*12"x12" Bright Tints*)
- **solid Paper Pizazz™:** dark green, burgundy, dark purple, medium purple (*Solid Jewel Tones*); ivory (*Plain Pastels*)
- **two ¹⁄₁₆" wide gold; 1 brown, 3 pink, 4 blue, 4 green, 6 light green ³⁄₁₆" wide eyelets:** Stamp Studio
- **22-gauge purple wire:** Artistic Wire, Ltd.™
- **pink decorating chalk:** Craf-T Products
- **³⁄₈" wide, 1" wide flower punches:** Marvy® Uchida
- **black pen:** Sakura 5mm Micron
- **foam adhesive tape:** Scotch® Brand
- **tracing paper, transfer paper**
- **page designer:** Lisa Garcia-Bergstedt

Shauna's ideas blossomed with this lovely page. She placed the tulip collage paper on a cutting surface and used an X-acto® knife to cut out the center tulip and part of its stem. She glued a 2½"x5" rectangle of sage vellum behind the cut-out tulip, then used foam tape to attach the tulip to the vellum. She matted the photo on sage vellum, outlined it in silver and glued it 2¼" from the page top and right sides. She cut out fourteen 1¾" squares, three 2⅛"x1¼" and one 1"x1¼" rectangles from the vellums, outlining each with the silver pen. She placed seven vellum squares on top of matching squares of tulip photos, then attached each to the page with an eyelet in each center. She tore the bottom edge of a 3"x4¼" rectangle of sage vellum, glued it above the tulips, then placed two pink vellum retangles on it and outlined each in silver. She tied the ribbon in a shoestring bow and glued it to the top pink vellum rectangle then journaled with the silver pen.

- **specialty Paper Pizazz™:** sage vellum, dark pink vellum, plum pink vellum, lavender vellum (*12"x12" Pastel Vellum Papers*); pastel pink vellum (*12"x12" Pastel Vellum Papers*, also by the sheet)
- **patterned Paper Pizazz™:** tulip collage (*Holidays & Seasons Collage Papers*)
- **4 pink, 16 green eyelets:** Stamp Studio
- **9" of ½" wide white sheer ribbon:** C.M. Offray & Son, Inc.
- **1" wide flower punch:** Marvy® Uchida
- **silver pen:** Sakura Gelly Roll
- **X-acto® knife, cutting surface:** Hunt Manufacturing Company
- **glue dots:** Glue Dots™ International LLC
- **foam adhesive tape:** Scotch® Brand
- **page designer:** Shauna Berglund-Immel

Shauna created a spectacular Oriental theme with tags and eyelets for this heirloom page. She used brown collage paper for a background, attached three small eyelets in each corner, then inserted thread through them as shown. She cut a 5¾"x7¾" rectangle of wrought iron gold paper, matted it on black and placed it behind a 6¾"x8¾" rectangle of tan vellum, outlined in gold pen. With an eyelet in each vellum corner, she inserted thread through them. She matted her photo on gold and black, then attached a round tag, with a center eyelet wrapped with fiber, to the lower right corner. She used an X-acto® knife to cut out the pink fans on the large tags and lifted each up. She matted all the tags on gold, inserted an eyelet at the tops with fiber and thread.

- **specialty Paper Pizazz™:** gold/black wrought iron, gold (*Metallic Gold*, also by the sheet); pastel tan vellum (*12"x12" Pastel Vellum Papers*, also by the sheet)
- **patterned Paper Pizazz™:** brown collage (*Masculine Collage Papers*)
- **solid Paper Pizazz™:** black (*Solid Jewel Tones*)
- **tags:** *Paper Pizazz™ Tag Art Cut-Outs™*
- **twenty ¹⁄₁₆", eight ⅛" brass eyelets:** Stamp Studio
- **black fibers:** Adornaments™
- **black decorating chalk:** Craf-T Products
- **metallic gold thread:** Wrights®
- **¹⁄₁₆", ⅛" wide circle punches:** Family Treasures, Inc.
- **gold, black pens:** Sakura Gelly Roll
- **X-acto® knife, cutting surface:** Hunt Manufacturing Company
- **glue dots:** Glue Dots™ International LLC
- **foam adhesive tape, clear adhesive tape:** Scotch® Brand
- **page designer:** Shauna Berglund-Immel

Fasteners—you might call them brads. They're great on a page!

Lisa used brass fasteners to create an upholstery look for this fabulous page. She began with a plaid background, then made a diagonal grid with ribbon. The fasteners were placed at intersecting points. She matted each photo on pale yellow; then one on pink flowers on yellow paper and the other on pink with words paper. Each was glued to the page with one corner tucked under a ribbon. Lisa used tags for journaling, with the ballerina and pink ribbon around one, then raffia around the other as shown. She inserted gold thread through the charms and locket with the ends tied around the fastener in the right corner. Lisa cut out items from the four motif patterned papers and tucked them behind the ribbons.

- **patterned Paper Pizazz™:** pink flowers on yellow, pink with words, pink/yellow plaid (*Mixing Light Papers*); letters, stamps, tickets, travel stickers (by the sheet)
- **solid Paper Pizazz™:** pale yellow (*Plain Pastels*)
- **ten 7/16" wide brass fasteners:** Hyglo/AmericanPin
- **ballerina, hearts, locket charms:** Creative Beginnings
- **pink, yellow decorating chalks:** Craf-T Products
- **1⅝"x3¼", 4¼"x2⅛" ivory tags:** Paper Reflections
- **8" of maize twistel raffia**
- **metallic gold embroidery thread:** DMC
- **8 yards of ¼" wide dark pink satin ribbon, 7" of ⅝" wide pink sheer ribbon:** C.M. Offray & Son, Inc.
- **black pen:** Sakura 5mm Micron
- **page designer:** Lisa Garcia-Bergstedt

Lisa arranged three brass fasteners to anchor the floral motifs to this lovely page. Lavender flowers on vellum was placed on white for a background. Lisa cut a 7⅞"x1" rectangle of lavender sponged, matted it on white and purple vellum; then inserted three fasteners as shown. The photo was matted on purple and vellum. Lisa used the punches to make seven flowers and circle centers from the various papers. She cut seven 5½"x⅛" strips from the green and glued one end to each flower. She wrapped one wire end around the stems seven times and looped the other wire end around the left fastener, so it appears to hang.

- **specialty Paper Pizazz™:** pastel purple vellum (*Pastel Vellum Papers*, also by the sheet)
- **patterned Paper Pizazz™:** white flowers on lavender vellum, lavender sponged (*Mixing Papers and Vellums*)
- **solid Paper Pizazz™:** purple, green (*Solid Jewel Tones*); oatmeal, mauve, peach, lavender (*Solid Muted Colors*); white (*Plain Pastels*)
- **three 7/16" wide brass fasteners:** Hyglo/AmericanPin
- **24-gauge metallic purple wire:** Artistic Wire, Ltd.™
- **1" flower, ¼" wide hole punches:** Family Treasures, Inc.
- **black pen:** Sakura 3mm Micron
- **page designer:** Lisa Garcia-Bergstedt

Shauna mapped her way to fun with this clever use of fasteners to mark her every move. She trimmed the road map paper and green vellum each into 5½"x12" rectangles and glued them near the left side of the road collage paper. She cut out three signs from the road signs paper, covered each in green vellum and used foam tape to attach them in the lower left corner of the page. She matted the photos on green. She inserted fasteners in the map rectangle, then used the black pen to write out the itinerary.

- **specialty Paper Pizazz**™: pastel green vellum (*12"x12" Pastel Vellum Papers*, also by the sheet)
- **patterned Paper Pizazz**™: road collage, road signs collage (*Vacation Collage Papers*); road map (*Our Vacation*, also by the sheet)
- **solid Paper Pizazz**™: green (*Solid Jewel Tones*)
- **four ⁵⁄₁₆" wide green fasteners:** Hyglo/ AmericanPin
- **black pen:** Sakura Gelly Roll
- **foam adhesive tape:** Scotch® Brand
- **page designer:** Shauna Berglund-Immel

Lisa fastened this precious moment in time with brass fasteners and gold wire for a stunning time-piece. She used vines on stripes for a background. She matted her photo on black and brown, then overlayed a 12"x1½" rectangle of white vellum, attached with a fastener at each end. She used the black pen to journal on the vellum strip. She cut a 4" wide circle from vines on black, matted it on brown and black, then used the gold pen to draw the clock face. She inserted the large fastener in the clock center, then used 6" lengths of wire to form to clock hands and wrapped the ends around the fastener as shown. She glued the clock to a 5½" square of gray floral, matted on black and brown with a fastener in each corner. She journaled on a rectangle of white vellum, attached with a fastener in each corner.

- **specialty Paper Pizazz**™: white vellum (by the sheet)
- **patterned Paper Pizazz**™: gray floral, vines on stripes, vines on black (*Mixing Heritage Papers*)
- **solid Paper Pizazz**™: brown (*Solid Muted Colors*); black (*Solid Jewel Tones*)
- **ten ³⁄₁₆", one ⁷⁄₁₆" wide brass fasteners:** Hyglo/ AmericanPin
- **20-gauge gold wire:** Artistic Wire, Ltd.™
- **gold, black pens:** Sakura Gelly Roll
- **page designer:** Lisa Garcia-Bergstedt

a timeless love...

Fasteners

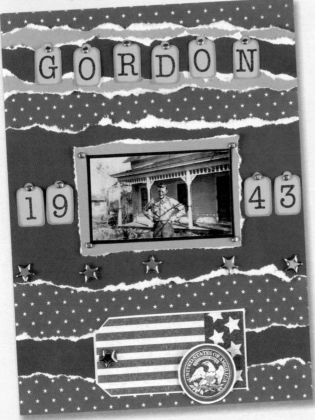

LeNae showed her patriotic flair with this heirloom photo. She used white stars on red paper for a background, then tore an 8½"x2" strip of tan, two 8½"x1" strips and a 8½"x4½" rectangle of blue and glued them to the page as shown. She cut out the letter and number tags to form the name and date then attached each tag with a round fastener. She cut out the flag tag, matted it on white and glued it to the page. The emblem tag was matted on white and attached to the flag tag with foam tape. LeNae inserted five star fasteners along the bottom edge of the center blue strip and one in the circle of the flag tag. She matted her photo on black, then tan and tore the edges. A fastener was inserted into each corner of the photo mat.

- **patterned Paper Pizazz™:** white stars on red (*Dots, Checks, Plaids & Stripes*)
- **solid Paper Pizazz™:** tan, blue (*Solid Muted Colors*); white (*Plain Pastels*)
- **tags:** *Paper Pizazz™ Tag Art Cut-Outs™*
- **fourteen ³⁄₁₆" wide round, six ½" wide silver star fasteners:** Hyglo/AmericanPin
- **⅛" wide circle punch:** McGill
- **black pen:** Sakura 15mm Micron
- **foam adhesive tape:** Scotch® Brand
- **page designer:** LeNae Gerig

LeNae got a little wild with this whimsical zoo page. She used clouds for a background, then cut a ½"x10½" strip and limbs from barnwood then glued the pieces to the right side to form a tree. She cut a 12"x2½" rectangle of grass, then tore the top edge to round one side to 1½" tall and glued it to the bottom edge of the page. She cut out the animal motifs, glued the birds to the tree, then cut the giraffe in half at the neck, gluing only the bottom half. She inserted a fastener to attach the giraffe bottom half and hippopotamus to the page so they swing. She matted the photos on two layers of solid colors, then glued them and the remaining motifs to the page as shown. She used the template to cut the letters from grass and journaled with the black pen.

- **patterned Paper Pizazz™:** 12"x12" grass, 12"x12" barnwood, 12"x12" clouds (by the sheet)
- **solid Paper Pizazz™:** blue, yellow, green, pink (*Plain Brights*); brown, tan (*Solid Muted Colors*); black (*Solid Jewel Tones*)
- **animal motifs:** (*Paper Pizazz™ Annie Lang's Big Cut-Outs™*)
- **two ³⁄₁₆" wide round gold fasteners:** Hyglo/AmericanPin
- **alphabet template:** Frances Meyer, Inc.® Fat Caps
- **black pen:** Zig® Millennium
- **page designer:** LeNae Gerig

LeNae created a fun theme around Maddie's flower photos. She used blue gingham for a background paper. For the pinwheels, she cut 3" squares each from the yellow patterned papers and the gingham colors. She glued the back of each yellow patterned square to a gingham patterned back, then transferred the pattern onto each to cut the pinwheel shapes and punch the holes. She folded one corner of each section inward to form a pinwheel and secured it in the center with a fastener. She cut ¼" wide strips of white in 3", 5½" and 9" lengths and glued a pinwheel to the top of each strip. She matted her photos on yellow, then overlapped them slightly on a 5⅝"x8½" rectangle of pink swirls, matted on white. She journaled with the black pen on white, matted it on green and used a fastener to attach it to the photo mat as shown.

- **patterned Paper Pizazz™**: bright tints pink swirls, bright tints pink gingham, bright tints blue gingham, bright tints green gingham, bright tints yellow gingham, bright tints yellow swirls (*12"x12" Bright Tints*, also by the sheet); bright tints plum gingham, bright tints yellow dots (*12"x12" Bright Tints*)
- **solid Paper Pizazz™**: yellow, green (*Plain Brights*); white (*Plain Pastels*)
- **eight ³⁄₁₆" wide round gold fasteners**: Hyglo/AmericanPin
- **⅛" wide circle punch**: McGill
- **black pen**: Zig® Millennium
- **tracing paper, transfer paper**
- **page designer**: LeNae Gerig

Lisa used ribbons, tulle and fasteners to stage this delightful production. White vellum was placed over pink gingham paper for a background. Lisa matted her photo on white, pink/yellow plaid and white again, then attached it to the page with a washer and fastener in each corner. She transferred the body, two arms and two legs onto hearts/words on pink paper and two slippers onto plaid, matting each slipper on white. She laced ribbon around each leg, sewed the tulle around the waist and glued the slippers to the legs. Lisa used fasteners to attach the body pieces, then punched a hole in the tops of the slippers and arms and threaded ribbon through each hole to the top of the page. The ballerina was attached to the page with foam tape. Lisa used the pens for journaling.

- **specialty Paper Pizazz™**: white vellum (by the sheet)
- **patterned Paper Pizazz™**: hearts/words on pink, pink/yellow plaid (*Mixing Light Papers*); soft tints pink gingham (*12"x12" Soft Tints*, also by the sheet)
- **solid Paper Pizazz™**: white (*Plain Pastels*)
- **eight silver fasteners, four silver washers**: Hyglo/AmericanPin
- **metallic silver thread, sewing needle**: Wrights®
- **1½ yards of ⅛" wide pink satin ribbon**: C.M. Offray & Son, Inc.
- **6" wide circle of white tulle with white flecks**
- **⅛" wide circle punch**: McGill
- **pink, black pen**: Sakura Gelly Roll
- **foam adhesive tape**: Scotch® Brand
- **tracing paper, transfer paper**
- **page designer**: Lisa Garcia-Bergstedt

She dances with such grace...

so softly like someone else is playing the strings. She was born to be a dancer and she will always be a princess.

Emma

Fibers

Arlene created a winter wonderland filled with textured fibers and vellum snowflakes. She used snowflake collage paper for a background. She cut a 6½"x8¾" white vellum rectangle and punched 15 holes along the top and bottom sides. She inserted alternating fibers through the holes from the back, then matted it on blue vellum. She matted her photo on blue vellum and glued it to the fiber mat. She journaled on white vellum and matted it on blue vellum. She punched two 1" snowflakes from blue vellum, glued one on each end of the vellum rectangle, then punched a hole in each snowflake and inserted fiber. She glued punched white vellum snowflakes on the left side of the page. Two eyelets were inserted below the snowflake motif and two more 1" from the bottom edge of the page. She inserted strands of fibers extending through the eyelets.

- **specialty Paper Pizazz™:** pastel blue vellum (*12"x12" Pastel Vellum Papers*, also by the sheet); white vellum (by the sheet)
- **patterned Paper Pizazz™:** blue snowflake collage (*Vacation Collage Papers*)
- **white, blue fibers:** Adornments™
- **four ⁵⁄₁₆" wide white eyelets:** Stamp Studio
- **½", 1", 1¼" wide snowflake punches:** Family Treasures, Inc.
- **⅛" wide circle punch:** Marvy® Uchida
- **page designer:** Arlene Peterson

Arlene pulled the colors from her photo, then used fibers to simulate the netting for this fun page. She chose teal marble for a background. She cut 7½"x11¼" and 2⅞"x11¼" rectangles of yellow and matted each on black. She tore 7¼"x11" and 2½"x11" rectangles from purple scuffed paper, then created frames by tearing out two 4¼"x4¾" rectangles from the larger purple rectangle and three 1½"x2¼" rectangles from the other purple rectangle, then used the remnants to make smaller torn-edge rectangles. She punched three holes on each side of the small frames and torn rectangles, and in each corner around the photo frames. She inserted the fiber strands to connect the rectangles to the frames and encircle the photos. Arlene journaled on rectangles of yellow, matted each on black and glued them between the frames.

- **patterned Paper Pizazz™:** purple scuffed, teal marble (*Great Jewel Backgrounds*)
- **solid Paper Pizazz™:** yellow (*Solid Bright Papers*)
- **solid black paper**
- **black fiber:** Adornments™
- **¹⁄₁₆" wide circle punch:** Marvy® Uchida
- **page designer:** Arlene Peterson

Lisa threaded strands of fiber for a stunning highlight to this elegant page. She cut 5"x10" rectangles each of white and ivory vellums, outlined them with the bronze pen, then drew flowers randomly on each. She glued them ⅜" apart on a brown collage paper background. She cut a 12"x1" strip of tan vellum, outlined it in bronze and attached it to the page bottom with an eyelet at each end. She matted her photo on dark brown, tan, then medium brown. She inserted three sets of eyelets ½" apart near the left side of the photo mat. Lisa placed strands of fibers along the left of the photo mat, then used other strands inserted through the eyelets to secure the fibers in place. She used the black pen for journaling on the vellums.

- **specialty Paper Pizazz™:** pastel tan vellum, tan, ivory vellum (*12"x12" Pastel Vellum Papers*, also by the sheet); white vellum (by the sheet)
- **patterned Paper Pizazz™:** brown collage (*Pretty Collage Papers*)
- **solid Paper Pizazz™:** tan, medium brown, dark brown (*Solid Muted Colors*)
- **brown fibers:** Adornaments™
- **eight ⁵⁄₁₆" wide gold eyelets:** Stamp Studio
- **bronze, black pens:** Sakura Gelly Roll
- **page designer:** Lisa Garcia-Bergstedt

Lisa used white and blue fibers to create a spectacular lattice effect for this fun page. She placed alternating fiber colors diagonally across the page, gluing the ends at the back. She matted her photo on white, then tri-dots on blue and again on white. She used foam tape to attach the photo mat to the center of the page. She die-cut the letters from tri-dots on blue, matted each on white and glued them along the top and bottom edges of the photo mat. She cut 14 snowman blocks and attached each with foam tape at intersecting points along the fiber lattice.

- **patterned Paper Pizazz™:** blue snowflake, tri-dots on blue, snowman blocks (*Mixing Christmas Papers*)
- **solid Paper Pizazz™:** white (*Plain Pastels*)
- **white, blue fibers:** Adornaments™
- **traveler letter die-cuts:** Accu/Cut® Systems
- **foam adhesive tape:** Scotch® Brand
- **page designer:** Lisa Garcia-Bergstedt

Flowers

LeNae captured a favorite moment with silk flowers for this exquisite page. She used the green/blue collage paper for a background. She mounted her photo on white and black, then vellum ferns. She cut 6"x8" rectangles from the lavender floral and purple papers then glued the backs together. She folded 1" inward on each corner, then folded it back and attached her matted photo inside. She used glue dots to place the flowers, ferns and grass blades in the lower left corner as shown. The white pen was used for journaling. It's such a lovely scene!

- **specialty Paper Pizazz™:** vellum ferns (*Vellum Papers*, also by the sheet)
- **patterned Paper Pizazz™:** green/blue collage (*Collage Papers*); lavender floral (*Muted Tints*)
- **solid Paper Pizazz™:** purple, black (*Solid Jewel Tones*); white (*Plain Pastels*)
- **silk flowers:** 9" tall grass; fern with seven 3"-5" fronds; four 2½" wide white orchids; four 1" wide lavender, eight 1" wide white baby's breath sprigs; one 1½" fuchsia hydrangea blossom
- **white pen:** Pentel Milky Gel Roller
- **glue dots:** Glue Dots™ International LLC
- **page designer:** LeNae Gerig

Lisa framed her precious photo with soft velvet flowers and vellums. She placed the blue collage paper with the floral border on a cutting surface and cut along the flowers to ½" from each side. She used the silver pen to outline the silhouette. She cut a 9⅜"x10" rectangle from the remaining collage paper, then cut out two floral motifs, squaring off the bottom and sides. She folded the edges around the top corners of the collage rectangle, then matted the collage rectangle on white vellum and outlined the edges in silver. She tucked the bottom edge of the mat behind the floral silhouette. She matted her photo on blue then white vellum, outlined the vellum edge in silver. She used glue dots to attach the flowers and leaves as shown.

- **specialty Paper Pizazz™:** white vellum (by the sheet)
- **patterned Paper Pizazz™:** blue floral/lace companion papers (*Pretty Collage Papers*)
- **solid Paper Pizazz™:** blue (*Solid Muted Colors*)
- **velvet flowers:** five ½" wide dark purple, eight ½" wide white blossoms, two ¾" wide green leaves
- **silver pen:** Sakura Gelly Roll
- **mini glue dots:** Glue Dots™ International LLC
- **X-acto knife, cutting surface:** Hunt Manufacturing Company
- **page designer:** Lisa Garcia-Bergstedt

Lisa preserved a wondrous moment with flowers and vellum. She chose purple floral collage for a background. She enlarged her photo and reversed the image to create a 9"x7½" rectangle and matted it on medium purple paper. She tore a 10½"x10" rectangle of purple vellum and glued it over the matted photo. She matted her original photo on light purple, then dark purple. She used the silver pen to write the bride and groom's names on a 2"x2½" rectangle of purple vellum. She used glue dots to attach 10 flower clusters around the vellum rectangle, with the leaves and vines forming a border along the bottom edge. She pulled petals from the remaining cluster and glued them randomly along the bottom edge of the page. The silver pen was used for journaling.

- **specialty Paper Pizazz™:** pastel purple vellum (*12"x12" Pastel Vellum Papers*, also by the sheet); white vellum (by the sheet)
- **patterned Paper Pizazz™:** purple floral collage (*Pretty Collage Papers*)
- **solid Paper Pizazz™:** light purple, medium purple, dark purple (*Solid Muted Colors*)
- **paper flowers:** eleven ¾" wide round lavender/ purple blossoms with many ⅜" wide round petals, three 1½" wide green silk leaves and seven brown curled vines
- **silver pen:** Sakura Gelly Roll
- **mini glue dots:** Glue Dots™ International LLC
- **page designer:** Lisa Garcia-Bergstedt

LeNae captured the essence of romance with soft rose petals for this lovely page. She began with peach moiré paper for a background, then cut a 3½"x11½" rectangle of muted roses, matted it on white and glued it to the right side of the page. Each photo was matted on white, then pink vellum. She journaled on a rectangle of pink vellum, matted it on white and used decorative scissors to trim the bottom edge. She punched two holes near the top edge, threaded the tulle strips through and knotted them in the center. She pulled apart the rose blossoms and glued the petals randomly on the page.

- **specialty Paper Pizazz™:** pastel pink vellum (*12"x12" Pastel Vellum Papers*, also by the sheet)
- **patterned Paper Pizazz™:** peach moiré, muted roses (by the sheet)
- **solid Paper Pizazz™:** white (*12"x12" Solid Pastel Papers*)
- **silk flowers:** one peach/ivory rose blossom with artificial dew drops, one pink/ivory rose blossom with artificial dew drops
- **two ½"x7" strips of white tulle**
- **mini-scallop decorative scissors:** Fiskars®
- **⅛" wide circle punch:** Family Treasures, Inc.
- **black pen:** Zig® Millennium
- **page designer:** LeNae Gerig

Hemp & String

Lisa roped in a great idea for using string in this delightful page. She used navy with stars for a background, then cut out the planks on the barnwood paper to create fence posts, trimming the tops with decorative scissors. Each post was matted on ivory, then attached along the page bottom with eyelets. The hat pattern (on page 48) was cut from black, matted on ivory and glued together as shown. Lisa used die-cuts to make the letters from brown, then matted each on ivory and red. The star were punched from yellow and glued to the letters as shown. A hole was punched into each star center and the hat as shown. One end of the string was inserted the hat hole from the back to the front and inserted into the other hat hole, pulling the end to meet with the remaining string 3" below the hat rim, slipping the pony bead onto both strands and knotting it to secure. Lisa threaded and wrapped the string through the holes in the letters, knotting it at

the end. Each photo was matted on ivory, with the edges torn and chalked. A torn rectangle of ivory was chalked and placed on the page with the fasteners.

- **patterned Paper Pizazz™:** navy with stars, barnwood (by the sheet)
- **solid Paper Pizazz™:** brown, yellow (*Solid Muted Colors*); black, red (*Solid Jewel Tones*); ivory (*Plain Pastels*)
- **four ³⁄₁₆" wide brass fasteners, 22 eyelets:** Hyglo/AmericanPin
- **hemp string, red pony bead:** Westrim® Crafts
- **brown decorating chalk:** Craf-T Products
- **schoolhouse letter die-cuts:** Accu/Cut® Systems
- **deckle decorative scissors:** Family Treasures, Inc.
- **¼", ½" wide star punches, ¹⁄₁₆" wide hole punch:** Marvy® Uchida
- **brown pen:** Sakura 5mm Micron
- **tracing paper, transfer paper**
- **page designer:** Lisa Garcia-Bergstedt

Arlene used hemp and eyelets to recreate a scenic memory, beginning with green leaf collage paper for a background. She matted her photo on gold, then green, leaving a ⁷⁄₁₆" border; then again on gold. She inserted eyelets ½" apart around the green border, then inserted two strands of hemp through each pair of eyelets. She cut four 2" squares of green, matted each on gold and inserted an eyelet in each corner. She punched four leaves from gold, glued one to each square, then threaded hemp through the eyelets. She journaled on gold, matted on green and gold.

- **specialty Paper Pizazz™:** gold (*Metallic Gold*, also by the sheet)
- **patterned Paper Pizazz™:** green leaf collage (*Vacation Collage Papers*)
- **solid Paper Pizazz™:** forest green (*Solid Jewel Tones*)
- **hemp:** Westrim® Crafts
- **64 gold eyelets:** Stamp Studio
- **1" leaf punch:** Family Treasures, Inc.
- **page designer:** Arlene Peterson

LeNae couldn't resist making her own kite, complete with string for this fun page. She trimmed ⅛" off each side of the clouds paper, then matted it on black. She cut two 4¾"x2¾" rectangles from the sandstone, then tore the top edges to form sand dunes. She matted her photos on black. She used the patterns to make the triangle shapes for the kite, glued them to the page as shown and attached a length of string between the kite and photo with glue dots. She cut a tail each from yellow, red and green, tied string around each and inserted the end behind the kite bottom. She journaled with the black pen.

- **patterned Paper Pizazz™:** clouds (*Vacation*, also by the sheet); blue dot, green diamonds (*Bright Tints*); sandstone (by the sheet)
- **solid Paper Pizazz™:** yellow, red, green (*Plain Brights*); black (*Solid Jewel Tones*)
- **hemp string:** Westrim® Crafts
- **tracing paper, transfer paper**
- **black pen:** Zig® Millennium
- **glue dots:** Glue Dots™ International LLC
- **page designer:** LeNae Gerig

Arlene created a rustic look wrapped in twine to frame this treasured photo. She used barnwood for a background. The photo was matted on black, denim and again on black for depth. Arlene inserted a large eyelet in each corner of the denim mat; then thread twine through the eyelets, knotting them at each corner. She cut 1"x11" and 1"x8½" strips of denim, matted each on black and glued them as shown. Arlene used a set of smaller eyelets at the end of each strip, then inserted twine through the holes, gluing the ends at the back. Arlene journaled on a 3½"x1" rectangle of ivory, matted it on black, denim and again on black. It was adhered to the page with foam tape as shown.

- **patterned Paper Pizazz™:** barnwood, denim (by the sheet)
- **solid Paper Pizazz™:** black (*Solid Jewel Tones*); ivory (*Plain Pastels*)
- **hemp:** Westrim® Crafts
- **eight ³⁄₁₆", four ¼" wide gold eyelets:** Stamp Studio
- **foam adhesive tape:** Scotch® Brand
- **page designer:** Arlene Peterson

Metal & Wire Mesh

Metal foils and meshes transformed Lisa's ideas into a work of art. And, it's easy to use in your pages. Lisa began with green swirls for a background. She matted her photo on green, copper, green brushstroke and green. She journaled on a 10⅝"x1" strip of white vellum, matted it on green brushstrokes, green and copper then attached it to the page with an eyelet at each end. Lisa traced the butterfly lower wings and body (see patterns on page 1) onto mesh and the upper wings onto copper foil, using the wood embossing tool to etch in the details and the punches for the holes. A heat gun was used to create the multi-colored designs on the mesh. Copper wire was used to wrap the body, with four beads threaded onto the last wrap and one at the end of each antennae loop. Lisa twisted two strands of wire to create the "trail" from the top left corner to the butterfly.

- **specialty Paper Pizazz™:** copper (*Heavy Metal Papers*); white vellum (by the sheet)
- **patterned Paper Pizazz™:** green swirl, green brushstroke (*Great Jewel Backgrounds*)
- **solid Paper Pizazz™:** hunter green (*Solid Muted Colors*)
- **WireForm® copper mesh, ArtEmboss™ copper foil, embossing tool:** American Art Clay Co., Inc.
- **24-gauge copper wire:** Artistic Wire, Ltd.™
- **metallic lavender seed beads:** Blue Moon Beads/ Elizabeth Ward & Co., Inc.
- **2 copper eyelets:** Stamp Studio
- **heat gun, heat-resistant surface**
- **tracing paper**
- **⅛", ¼" ½" wide circle punches:** Marvy® Uchida
- **foam adhesive tape:** Scotch® Brand
- **copper, black pens:** Sakura Gelly Roll
- **cursive computer font:** Creating Keepsakes
- **page designer:** Lisa Garcia-Bergstedt

Lisa captured the essence Molly's seaside visit with a clever use of metals. She used the patterns on page 47 to create the anchor and portholes then added the fasteners and hemp as shown. She wrapped copper foil around the wooden dowel for added interest. She cut the lifesaver from white, wrapped ribbon around it and threaded hemp along the outer edge. The alphabet template and sign were cut from barnwood and matted on purple. Foam tape was used to attach the letters and lifesaver.

- **patterned Paper Pizazz™:** white dots on lavender, lavender blue swirl (*Mixing Light Papers*); barnwood (by the sheet)
- **solid Paper Pizazz™:** purple (*Solid Jewel Tones*); white (*Plain Pastels*)
- **24 silver, 1 gold ⅛" wide fasteners:** Hyglo/AmericanPin
- **2 gold eyelets:** Stamp Studio
- **ArtEmboss™ aluminum foil:** American Art Clay Co., Inc.
- **26" of hemp:** Westrim® Crafts
- **8" of ¼" wide lavender satin ribbon:** C.M. Offray & Son, Inc.
- **¼"x12" wooden dowel**
- **glue dots:** Glue Dots™ International LLC
- **alphabet template:** Frances Meyer, Inc.® Fat Caps
- **black pen:** Sakura Gelly Roll
- **page designer:** Lisa Garcia-Bergstedt

Shauna used the tools of the trade to create this 3-dimensional masculine theme page. The tool collage companion paper was the inspiration for adding the wire mesh rectangle. Shauna used gold thread to sew the top and bottom mesh edges to the paper, then inserted a fastener in each corner. She cut out the tool shapes from the tool collage paper and used glue dots to secure them to the mesh. She bent two 1½" lengths of copper wire into "S" shapes to hang two of the tool shapes, then added a mini fastener to each of the other tools. The screwdriver was glued to ivory vellum, torn to form an oval, and used for journaling. The photo is matted on silver.

- **specialty Paper Pizazz™**: ivory vellum (*Pastel Vellum Papers*, also by the sheet); silver (*Metallic Silver*, also by the sheet)
- **patterned Paper Pizazz™**: tool collage, tool collage companion (*Masculine Collage Papers*)
- **WireForm® silver mesh:** American Art Clay Co., Inc.
- **six ⅛", four ¼" wide gold fasteners:** Hyglo/AmericanPin
- **24-gauge copper wire:** Artistic Wire, Ltd.™
- **gold thread:** Westrim® Crafts
- **sewing needle**
- **black pen:** Sakura Gelly Roll
- **glue dots:** Glue Dots™ International LLC
- **page designer:** Shauna Berglund-Immel

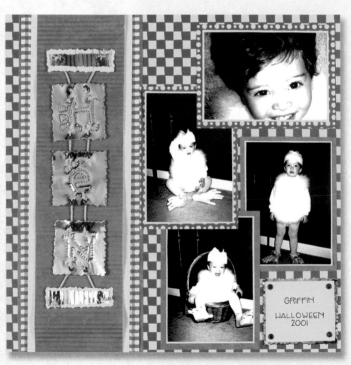

Lisa created a delightful mix of patterned papers, photos and metal signs to remember Griffin's Halloween. She chose checks for a bright background, then matted two photos on red sponged and two more on the dots paper. She overlapped them on the page for added interest. She crimped a 3"x12" strip of red sponged, matted it on yellow, gingham and red sponged, trimming the top and bottom edges even. Three 2" squares and two 2½"x½" strips were cut from foil using decorative scissors. Lisa embossed each foil square with a letter, then inserted a set of eyelets along each top and bottom. The foil strips were crimped and matted on yellow, with an eyelet at each end. Lisa used strands of twistel to connect them as shown. She journaled on a 2⅜"x2" rectangle of yellow, glued it to foil and secured it to the page with an eyelet in each corner.

- **patterned Paper Pizazz™**: yellow dots on red, red/yellow gingham, red/yellow checks (*Bright Tints*); red sponged (*Mixing Bright Papers*)
- **solid Paper Pizazz™**: yellow (*Solid Pastel Papers*)
- **ArtEmboss™ aluminum foil, embossing tool:** American Art Clay Co., Inc.
- **20 red eyelets:** Stamp Studio
- **20" of maize twistel**
- **paper crimper:** Marvy® Uchida
- **deckle decorative scissors:** Fiskars®
- **black pen:** Sakura 5mm Micron
- **page designer:** Lisa Garcia-Bergstedt

Micro Beads & Glitter

MY First Egg Hunt

Hailey
March 2002

Arlene made Hailey's first egg hunt sparkle with micro beads and glitter. She used blue swirls for a background. She cut three 1½" wide strips of green gingham and cut along the top of each to simulate grass, then matted each on white vellum with torn edges and layered the strips from the bottom edge. She matted her photos on white vellum, leaving ⅝" wide borders on the left and right sides then glued ½" wide strips of micro beads to the vellum borders. She cut nine egg shapes from white vellum and glued micro beads and glitter to each in random patterns, then glued the eggs in the layered grass strips. She computer journaled on a 12"x2" strip of white vellum, tearing the long edges to form the top banner and glued it to a green gingham strip.

- **specialty Paper Pizazz™:** white vellum (by the sheet)
- **patterned Paper Pizazz™:** bright tints blue swirls, bright tints green gingham (*12"x12" Bright Tints*, also by the sheet)
- **turquoise, red and green mix micro beads; pink glitter beads; purple treasure beads; Terrifically Tacky Tape™:** Art Accents
- **page designer:** Arlene Peterson

Lisa created a spectacular effect with mini marbles that roll with movement within their sealed pouch. She began with the boats collage paper for a background. She cut out the boat patterns (see inside the back cover) from blue, red and white papers then used foam tape to attach them to the page. She cut two 5" squares from a sheet protector and glued three sides together, inserted the mini marbles, then sealed the top. For her frame, she cut a 6" square from the boat collage companion paper, with the center cut out to form a 1" wide frame; then cut a 6⅛" square of white and glued her photo in the center. She placed the marble pouch on top of the photo, then the frame on top of the pouch and used foam tape around the sides to complete this wonderful frame.

- **patterned Paper Pizazz™:** boats on the lake companion set collage (*Holidays & Seasons Collage Papers*); sandstone (by the sheet)
- **solid Paper Pizazz™:** blue (*Solid Muted Colors*); red (*Solid Jewel Tones*); white (*Solid Pastel Papers*)
- **clear, clear blue mini marbles:** Halcraft USA
- **foam adhesive tape:** Scotch® Brand
- **black pens:** Sakura 5mm, 3mm Micron
- **a sheet protector**
- **page designer:** Lisa Garcia-Bergstedt

Those lazy, hazy, crazy, days of...
Summer
Lake Billy Chinook – July 2001

Griffin at play

Lisa discovered a treasure of possibilities using beads for texture and color. She journaled on a 3¼"x12" strip of white vellum, tore the right edge and placed the strip even with the left edge of the palm tree collage paper. She inserted an eyelet in each top corner of the vellum strip. She used the white pen to outline the palm tree silhouettes, then cut out the bottom 1½" silhouette and slipped a 12"x1½" strip of sandstone with the top edge torn behind the palms. She used tacky tape to cover the bottom edge of the sandstone strip, then covered it with gold micro and treasure beads plus a few green beads. She die-cut the letters, then attached tacky tape and covered the top halves with blue micro beads and the bottom halves with blue treasure beads. The letters were attached to the page with foam tape. Lisa matted her photo on blue, then gold and used the black pen for journaling.

- **specialty Paper Pizazz™**: white vellum (by the sheet); gold (*Metallic Gold*, also by the sheet)
- **patterned Paper Pizazz™**: palm tree collage (*Vacation Collage Papers*); sandstone (by the sheet)
- **solid Paper Pizazz™**: light blue (*Solid Muted Colors*)
- **turquoise, gold mix micro beads; blue, gold, green mix treasure beads; Terrifically Tacky Tape™**: Art Accents
- **two ¼" wide silver eyelets:** Stamp Studio
- **schoolhouse letter die-cuts:** Accu/Cut® Systems
- **foam adhesive tape:** Scotch® Brand
- **white, black pens:** Sakura Gelly Roll
- **page designer:** Lisa Garcia-Bergstedt

micro beads on flowers →

Susan created a stunning Bargello pattern with micro beads for this lovely page. She began with lavender gingham with flowers for a background, then glued a 10½" purple vellum square in the center. She used the silver pen to add a loopy line design as a border. Susan formed four 5" squares, alternating ½"-1" widths of floral and stripes papers. She cut 1/16"-1/8" wide strips of tacky tape and placed them between the patterned strips, then poured micro beads on top, gently brushing away any excess. She placed the squares as shown. She matted her photo on lavender, then pink vellum and outlined the edge in silver pen. She journaled on a lavender square, matted on floral and pink vellum and outlined in silver. She punched flowers from the vellums and glued micro beads to each center.

- **specialty Paper Pizazz™**: pastel purple vellum, pastel pink vellum (*12"x12" Pastel Vellum Papers*, also by the sheet)
- **patterned Paper Pizazz™**: pink/blue/orange floral, lavender gingham with flowers, lavender/green/yellow stripe (*Mixing Baby Papers*)
- **solid Paper Pizazz™**: lavender (*12"x12" Solid Pastel Papers*)
- **pink micro beads; Terrifically Tacky Tape™**: Art Accents
- **1" wide flower punch:** Family Treasures, Inc.
- **silver pen:** Sakura Gelly Roll
- **page designer:** Susan Cobb

Miniatures

Miniatures were just the thing to make this special page. Lisa designed all the items fit for two girlfriends and included them on page 48. She started with a background of yellow dots on green, then matted her photo on yellow, floral print on stripes and yellow. She printed the text of a treasured letter on yellow and matted it on gingham. A title box was printed on yellow and matted on the flowers & dots paper. Lisa used the papers as shown for the bikini, dress, purse and flip-flops. She unrolled the raffia for the hat. She used foam tape inside the purse, flip-flops and bikini for dimension. Lisa braided three 5" strands of burgundy ribbon and wrapped it around the hat, then glued the ribbon roses on top. She threaded white seed beads to make a necklace. Lavender ribbon was wrapped around the dress waist and tied in a bow in back with purple seed beads sewn in the center. More ribbon is glued along the dress hem.

- **patterned Paper Pizazz™:** yellow dots on green, floral print on stripes, pink/yellow gingham. flowers/dots on yellow (*Mixing Heritage Papers*)
- **solid Paper Pizazz™:** bright pink (*Solid Bright Papers*); pale yellow, ivory (*Plain Pastels*)
- **6 purple, 60 white seed beads:** Blue Moon Beads/ Elizabeth Ward & Co., Inc.
- **lavender thread:** Westrim® Crafts
- **30" of lavender, 26" of burgundy, 4" of pink ¹⁄₁₆" wide satin ribbon, three ³⁄₈" wide ivory ribbon roses:** C.M. Offray & Son, Inc.
- **8" of maize twistel raffia**
- **mini glue dots:** Glue Dots™ International LLC
- **foam adhesive tape:** Scotch® Brand
- **catfish script computer font:** Creating Keepsakes
- **tracing paper, transfer paper**
- **page designer:** Lisa Garcia-Bergstedt

LeNae dressed up this page with country charm. The sunflowers on blue paper made a perfect background for building a fence from strips of barnwood, matted on black. LeNae matted her photo on black, then blue plaid and again on black, leaving a 2" border on the bottom. The white pen was used for journaling and making stitch marks. She cut the scarecrow patterns (see inside the back cover) from the papers as shown and attached the raffia and hat with glue dots.

- **patterned Paper Pizazz™:** sunflowers on blue diamonds, blue plaid, yellow plaid with sunflowers (*Mixing Soft Patterned Papers*); barnwood, denim, burlap (*Country*, also by the sheet)
- **solid Paper Pizazz™:** ivory (*Plain Pastels*); black (*Solid Jewel Tones*)
- **2" wide straw hat, 24" of raffia:** Westrim® Crafts
- **pink, brown, orange decorative chalks:** Craf-T Products
- **white pen:** Pentel Milky Gel Roller
- **black pen:** Zig® Millennium
- **glue dots:** Glue Dots™ International LLC
- **tracing paper, transfer paper**
- **page designer:** LeNae Gerig

Shauna hung this delightful page with miniature clothespins. She began with blue diamonds for a background. The photo was matted on white, mesh then white again. Shauna computer journaled on white and matted each as shown. She thread strands of thread through each button and used glue dots to adhere them to a 4"x5" rectangle of white, matted on mesh. She die-cut three stars, matted each on white and trimmed the edges with decorative scissors. An eyelet was inserted at each side point, ribbon threaded through the holes and knotted at each end with a clothespin glued at the top corners.

- **patterned Paper Pizazz™:** yellow mesh, yellow dots on blue diamonds (*Mixing Bright Papers*)
- **solid Paper Pizazz™:** blue, white (*Plain Pastels*)
- **three 1" spring clothespins:** Forster Manufacturing, Inc.
- **four ⅝" wide yellow buttons**
- **6 silver eyelets:** Stamp Studio
- **star #2 die-cut:** Accu/Cut® Systems
- **16" of ¹⁄₁₆" wide white satin ribbon:** Wrights®
- **periwinkle embroidery thread:** DMC
- **mini-scallop decorative scissors:** Fiskars®
- **glue dots:** Glue Dots™ International LLC
- **foam adhesive tape:** Scotch® Brand
- **page designer:** Shauna Berglund-Immel

Visions of sugarplums danced on the page with Lauren's first Christmas photos. LeNae began her festive page with dot paper, then glued a ⅜" wide white strip near the top edge and used the black pen to draw a loopy line on it. She used the template to cut out letters from the stripes paper, glued them on a 8½"x1⅜" white rectangle and matted it on red then black. She used the pen to outline the letters. LeNae used tape to attach the candy cane cords to the back of the mat, then glued it to the page as shown. She matted each photo on white, red and black, then glued them as shown to a 12"x7¾" rectangle of peppermints, matted on white. She journaled on a white rectangle, matted it on red then black and glued it overlapping onto a photo. What a treat!

- **patterned Paper Pizazz™:** red with white dot, red/white stripes (*Christmas Time*); peppermints (*Yummy Papers*)
- **solid Paper Pizazz™:** red (*Plain Brights*); white (*12"x12" Solid Pastel Papers*); black (*Solid Jewel Tones*)
- **six 2" tall mini red/white plastic candy cane ornaments with gold cord**
- **mini-scallop decorative scissors:** Fiskars®
- **alphabet template:** Frances Meyer, Inc.® Fat Caps
- **black pen:** Zig® Millennium
- **clear adhesive tape:** Scotch® Brand
- **page designer:** LeNae Gerig

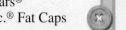

Pom Poms & Wiggle Eyes

Wiggle eyes add whimsy as Shauna used them to create cute bunnies for this adorable page. She matted rectangles of green and blue mesh papers on an 8½"x11" white sheet, then rectangles of blue and green ginghams on a 5⅜"x7⅛" rectangle of white. Shauna matted Kaelin's photo on white, glued it centered on the gingham mat, then glued an 8⅛"x½" strip of blue dots matted on white near the green mesh bottom and glued the mat on a blue gingham background. She cut the bunny (see inside the back cover) from brown, then cut three more bunny faces. She used the patterns for the vest, pocket and inner ears and used punches for the hearts. She cut the ribbon in quarters and tied each in a shoestring bow. She used the thread for the whiskers and glued wiggle eyes to complete each bunny face. She added details with the pens.

- **patterned Paper Pizazz™**: bright tints blue gingham, bright tints green gingham, bright tints green mesh (*12"x12" Bright Tints*, also by the sheet); bright tints blue dots, bright tints blue mesh (*12"x12" Bright Tints*)
- **solid Paper Pizazz™**: brown (*Solid Muted Colors*); pink, white (*Plain Pastels*)
- **4 sets of wiggle eyes**: Westrim® Crafts
- **8 white seed beads**: Blue Moon Beads/Elizabeth Ward & Co., Inc.
- **bunny die-cut**: Accu/Cut® Systems
- **1 yard of ¼" wide white sheer ribbon with satin edges**: C.M.Offray & Son, Inc.
- **white embroidery thread**: DMC
- **¼", 1¼" wide heart punches**: McGill
- **white pen**: Pentel Milky Gel Roller
- **black pen**: Sakura Gelly Roll
- **glue dots**: Glue Dots™ International LLC
- **foam adhesive tape**: Scotch® Brand
- **tracing paper, transfer paper**
- **page designer**: Shauna Berglund-Immel

Pretty pink pom poms added the perfect touch to LeNae's page. She chose pink buttons on plaid paper for a background, then matted each photo on green, pink gingham and white. She matted a 2½"x12" strip of pink gingham on green, then tore three 2½" squares of purple vellum, turned them on point and glued them on the strip. She used glue dots to attach the pom poms in heart shapes on the top and bottom squares and on a journaling rectangle of green. She journaled on white rectangles and matted each on pink.

- **specialty Paper Pizazz™**: pastel purple vellum (*12"x12" Pastel Vellum Papers*, also by the sheet)
- **patterned Paper Pizazz™**: pink buttons on plaid, small pink gingham (*Mixing Baby Papers*)
- **solid Paper Pizazz™**: light green, pink, white (*12"x12" Solid Pastel Papers*)
- **135 pink 5mm pom poms**: Westrim® Crafts
- **black pen**: Zig® Writer
- **mini glue dots**: Glue Dots™ International LLC
- **page designer**: LeNae Gerig

Pom Poms & Wiggle Eyes

Shauna wasn't scared to let her imagination go wild with this fun set of pages. She used multiple sets of wiggle eyes to set the tone for fun, with black and white photos adding to her holiday theme. Shauna began with the Halloween collage set of patterned papers for the backgrounds. She placed the tombstone page on a cutting surface and used an X-acto® knife to cut out the silhouettes along the tops of the five center tombstones, then placed a silhouette photo behind it. Shauna used the spiderweb patterns as a guide to create spiderwebs by stitching the thread on each page. She journaled on rectangles of white, matted on black. She completed the scene with Punch-Outs™ and wiggle eyes as shown.

- **patterned Paper Pizazz™:** graveyard collage, haunted house collage (*Holidays & Seasons Collage Papers*)
- **solid Paper Pizazz™:** black (*Solid Jewel Tones*); white (*Plain Pastels*)
- **Paper Pizazz™ motifs:** spider, ghost (*Fall & Halloween Punch-Outs™*)
- **10 sets of wiggle eyes:** Westrim® Crafts
- **white embroidery thread:** DMC
- **sewing needle**
- **white pen:** Sakura Gelly Roll
- **foam adhesive tape:** Scotch® Brand
- **X-acto® knife, cutting surface:** Hunt Manufacturing Company
- **toggle computer font:** Creating Keepsakes
- **page designer:** Shauna Berglund-Immel

LeNae chose tiny pom poms to embellish Lauren's baby photo. She cut 8½"x3" yellow diamonds, 8½"x5" yellow dots and an 8½"x3" of yellow checks then glued onto white for a bright background. She matted a 7⅛"x8¾" of green stripes on white and glued it to the page center. She matted her photo on white, then punched photo corners from yellow checks. She used glue dots to attach one yellow and six white pom poms to each photo corner. She cut 1¾" squares each from yellow dots, checks and diamonds then glued them to a 6"x2" rectangle of white. She repeated the process for attaching the pom poms, forming a flower on each square. She used the black pen to journal and make dots in the square corners.

- **patterned Paper Pizazz™:** yellow dot, yellow check, yellow diamonds, green stripe (*Bright Tints*)
- **solid Paper Pizazz™:** white (*Plain Pastels*)
- **42 white, 7 yellow 5mm pom poms:** Westrim® Crafts
- **scallop photo corner punch:** Marvy® Uchida
- **black pen:** Zig® Millennium
- **mini glue dots:** Glue Dots™ International LLC
- **page designer:** LeNae Gerig

Lauren at 3 months

Ribbon

Ribbons are a lovely way to add sophisticated elegance to your scrapbook pages. Susan cut a vellum heart pocket with a braided ribbon handle that's easy to make. She cut two large hearts (on page 47) and glued the sides together. She cut three 15" lengths of ribbon, taped them together at one end and braided them. The end was inserted it into a punched hole made inside the heart left side, then the tape was removed and ribbon ends were placed between the hearts. The remaining ribbon was tied in a shoestring bow. Susan used the flower punch to make pink vellum flowers to cover a small heart shape of pink vellum. She applied glue to each flower center with a stylus, then poured the micro beads over it and glued it to a vellum dots heart as shown. She used the vellums to mat the photo and glued it to the page.

- **specialty Paper Pizazz™:** pink floral bordered paper, pink floral vellum, pink swirl/leaf vellum, white dotted vellum (*Mixing Papers & Vellums*); dark pink vellum (*Pastel Vellum Papers*)
- **solid Paper Pizazz™:** white (*Plain Pastels*)
- **1½ yards of ¼" wide pink satin ribbon:** C.M. Offray & Son, Inc.
- **metallic pink micro beads:** Halcraft USA
- **⅜" wide flower, ¼" wide circle punches:** Fiskars®
- **Keep A Memory™ Adhesive:** Therm O Web
- **stylus, foam pad**
- **silver pen:** Sakura Gelly Roll
- **page designer:** Susan Cobb

vellum flower with micro beads

Lisa chose to wrap her wedding day memories with ribbons. Yellow dots paper made a soft background. Each photo was matted on ivory then pink. One of the smaller photos was matted once more on tan. A 16" ribbon length was glued to the left side, with the upper portion rolled in three layers and a "V" cut into each end. The three small photos are placed along the ribbon with foam tape on the left and right sides. Lisa matted her wedding invitation on pink and ivory. She punched two holes near the top. She cut a "V" into each end of the remaining ribbon, inserted it into the holes from the front, and pulled them the back, then re-inserted each end in the opposite hole back to the front. The large photo was glued overlapping the invitation.

- **patterned Paper Pizazz™:** soft tints yellow dots (*12"x12" Soft Tints*, also by the sheet)
- **solid Paper Pizazz™:** pink, ivory, tan (*Solid Muted Colors*)
- **24" of 1½" wide pale yellow satin ribbon with pink edges:** C.M. Offray & Son, Inc.
- **¼" wide circle punch:** Marvy® Uchida
- **wedding invitation**
- **page designer:** Lisa Garcia-Bergstedt

Arlene created a captivating theme with ribbon and metallic silver. She used silver/purple flourishes paper for a stunning background and matted her photo on silver, purple vellum, more silver and attached an eyelet in each corner. She inserted the narrow ribbon through the eyelets to form a frame. She matted a 1"x12" strip of vellum on silver and attached it with an eyelet at the top and bottom. Three 1¾"x2¼" rectangles of vellum were matted on silver, then three large eyelets were attached to each rectangle to form a triangle. Arlene inserted ribbon through the eyelets, making ribbon flowers. A rhinestone was glued in the center of each, with two leaves punched from silver attached at the bottom with foam tape. She glued the three rect-angles along the vellum strip. Arlene used vellum for journaling, matted it on silver and inserted an eyelet in each corner. She threaded ribbon into the eyelets and added a silver leaf at each end.

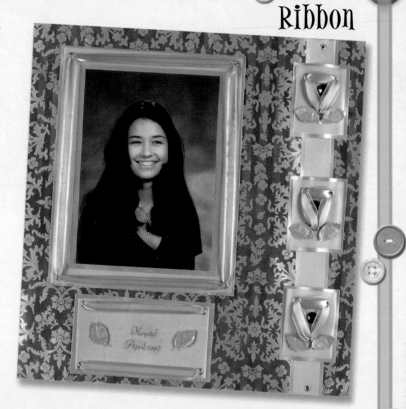

- **specialty Paper Pizazz™:** silver/purple flourishes, silver (*Metallic Silver*, also by the sheet); pastel purple vellum (*12"x12" Pastel Vellum Papers*, also by the sheet)
- **18" of ½" wide, 44" of ¼" wide lavender sheer/ satin ribbon:** C.M. Offray & Son, Inc.
- **ten ³⁄₁₆", nine ¼" wide silver eyelets:** Stamp Studio
- **three ⅜" wide purple acrylic rhinestones:** Westrim® Crafts
- **small leaf punch:** Marvy® Uchida
- **silver pen:** Pentel Hybrid Gel Roller
- **foam adhesive tape:** Scotch® Brand
- **page designer:** Arlene Peterson

LeNae used sheer ribbons to create her pretty ballerina theme. She began with muted roses paper for a background, then tore a diagonal line across the pink gingham to create a 2¼"-4" wide opening as shown. She punched holes along each gingham torn edge and placed the gingham halves on top of the muted roses paper. Then she wrapped the center of the ⅞" wide ribbon around the lower right corner and inserted the ends through the holes, lac-ing the ends to the upper left corner and tied it in a shoestring bow. She matted her photo on a torn-edge ivory rectangle, then matted it again on pink vellum, with torn edges. She punched two holes ¼" apart in each corner of the ivory, then threaded 3" lengths of the ⅝" wide ribbon through the holes and knotted each in the center. She repeated the process for her journal box.

- **specialty Paper Pizazz™:** pastel pink vellum (*12"x12" Pastel Vellum Papers*, also by the sheet)
- **patterned Paper Pizazz™:** soft tints pink gingham (*12"x12" Soft Tints*, also by the sheet); muted roses (by the sheet)
- **solid Paper Pizazz™:** ivory (*Plain Pastels*)
- **2½ yards of ⅞" wide, 1⅓ yards of ⅝" wide ivory sheer ribbon:** C.M. Offray & Son, Inc.
- **⅛" wide circle punch:** McGill
- **black pen:** Zig® Millennium
- **page designer:** LeNae Gerig

Ribbon

Ribbons tied Lisa's wedding theme together for a spectacular effect. She began with yellow stripes for a background, then matted her photo on white, ivory and pale yellow. She cut the cake from white cardstock (see patterns on page 47), then chalked the leaves green. She used sheer ribbon to create a lattice on the lower cake tier, gluing the ends only; then wrapped one length each around the top two tiers. She trimmed the layers with cord and pearls as shown, then glued satin roses as shown. Pink chalk is brushed around the ribbons. She cut two 7" lengths of sheer ribbon, folded each in an "L" shape in the top left and lower right corners then glued a rose in each corner. The black pen was used for journaling.

- **patterned Paper Pizazz™**: pale yellow diagonal stripes (*Soft Florals & Patterns*)
- **solid Paper Pizazz™**: yellow, ivory (*Plain Pastels*)
- **solid white cardstock**
- **2 yards of ¼" wide beige sheer ribbon; ⅔ yard of ivory satin cord; ⅔ yard of white fused pearls; 26 ivory ribbon roses with green ribbon leaves:** C.M. Offray & Son, Inc.
- **wedding cake die-cut:** Ellison® Craft & Design
- **green, pink decorating chalks:** Craf-T Products
- **black pen:** Sakura 5mm Micron
- **E-6000 glue:** Eclectic Products, Inc.
- **mini glue dots:** Glue Dots™ International LLC
- **foam adhesive tape:** Scotch® Brand
- **tracing paper, transfer paper**
- **page designer:** Lisa Garcia-Bergstedt

Susan wrapped this lovely page in ribbons. She used lavender fleur de lis paper for a background. She matted her photo on lavender paper and purple vellum, then outlined the edge with the silver pen. She placed the vellum on a cutting surface and used the X-acto® knife to make four ⁵/₁₆" tall slits along the top and bottom, then threaded a 5" length of ribbon through the slits as shown. She tied two shoestring bows from 10" lengths of ribbon and glued them on top. She used the patterns to make nested motifs as shown, punched a set of holes in each center and tied a 3" length of ribbon through the holes. She used the silver pen to journal on rectangles of purple vellum, then outlined each in silver.

- **specialty Paper Pizazz™**: pastel purple vellum (*12"x12" Pastel Vellum Papers*, also by the sheet)
- **patterned Paper Pizazz™**: lavender stripes, lavender paisley, light lavender floral, lavender fleur de lis (*Muted Tints*)
- **solid Paper Pizazz™**: lavender (*Plain Pastels*)
- **template:** *Paper Flair™ Nested Shapes Template*
- **1⅓ yards of ¼" wide lavender satin ribbon:** C.M. Offray & Son, Inc.
- **⅛" wide circle punch:** Fiskars®
- **silver pen:** Sakura Gelly Roll
- **X-acto® knife, cutting surface:** Hunt Mfg. Company
- **page designer:** Susan Cobb

LeNae used ribbon to add a romantic touch to Jason and Keri's wedding portrait. She tore a 1" wide section from the left side of the wedding words paper, then glued a 5"x12" rectangle of white roses behind it, so the roses appear through the torn gap. She punched four holes on each side of the torn gap, then inserted 9" lengths of ribbon through each pair of holes and knotted each in the center. She matted her photo on gold, then white, trimming the edges with decorative scissors. She glued the matted photo centered on a 5⅛"x6½" rectangle of tan vellum. She used the white pen to write the names in the lower right corner of the vellum.

- **specialty Paper Pizazz™:** pastel tan vellum (*Pastel Vellum Papers*, also by the sheet); gold (*Metallic Gold*, also by the sheet)
- **patterned Paper Pizazz™:** white roses (*Our Wedding Day*, also by the sheet); wedding words (by the sheet)
- **solid Paper Pizazz™:** white (*Plain Pastels*)
- **1 yard of 1½" wide ivory satin ribbon with wire edges:** C.M. Offray & Son, Inc.
- **mini antique decorative scissors:** Family Treasures, Inc.
- **¼" wide circle punch:** McGill
- **white pen:** Pentel Milky Gel Roller
- **page designer:** LeNae Gerig

LeNae adorned this lovely page with ribbons to match Alexis' dress and hairbow. She layered a 6"x11" blue floral rectangle and a 5½"x11" dark blue paisley rectangle, both with the left edges torn, even with the right side of the light blue paisley background paper. She matted her photo on white, then punched four flower photo corners from light blue paisley and white then four circles of blue for the flower centers. She cut a 2¼" square from blue stripes, matted it on white; then glued a 1¾" square of white vellum at an angle on top. She tied 9" of sheer ribbon into a shoestring bow and glued it to the top left corner of the vellum square. She tied three knots in the remaining ribbons and glued them to the left side of the page.

- **specialty Paper Pizazz™:** white vellum (by the sheet)
- **patterned Paper Pizazz™:** blue stripe, dark blue paisley, light blue paisley, dark blue floral (*Soft Muted Tints*)
- **solid Paper Pizazz™:** white (*Plain Pastels*)
- **24" of ⅝" wide white sheer, 12" of ⅛" wide light blue satin ribbon:** C.M. Offray & Son, Inc.
- **⅛" wide circle, ⅝" wide flower photo corner punches:** Marvy® Uchida
- **black pen:** Zig® Millennium
- **page designer:** LeNae Gerig

Rolled Paper

Rolled paper opened a whole new way to frame photos. Lisa matted a sheet of tan vellum stripes on white for a subtle background. She cut an 8½"x1" strip from the tan leaves on beige paper, matted it on white, with a 1⁄16" border on the bottom edge and attached it to the page top with an eyelet at each end. The title is ¾" white squares, matted on brown with copped pen letters. Holes were punched on each side, strung on wire and wrapped around the eyelets. The squares were strung together on wire inserted through the holes and wrapped around the eyelets on the top strip. She cut out the center of a 4⅞"x5⅝" rectangle of white, to form a ⅜" wide frame and used foam tape to attach over the photo. A 6"x¼" strip of white was centered on the top of a 5¼"x1" of white and placed below the photo frame, with chalking added for detail. For the

shade, Lisa glued a 4½"x5" rectangle of tan vellum leaves to the bottom edge of a 4½"x10" rectangle of white; then used decorative scissors to trim the bottom edge and inserted an eyelet as shown. She wrapped strands of thread to form a tassle and tied it to the eyelet. She tightly rolled the top of the white paper shade around a 20" length of wire until 3½" was remaining and glued it to secure, then twirled the wire ends. She attached the rolled portion to the frame top with foam tape. Wire was used to form the words along the bottom of the page, notice they're secured with eyelets.

- **patterned Paper Pizazz™:** tan vellum stripes, tan vellum leaves, tan leaves on beige (*Mixing Papers & Vellums*)
- **solid Paper Pizazz™:** brown (*Solid Muted Colors*); white (*Plain Pastels*)
- **7 copper eyelets:** Stamp Studio
- **tan decorating chalks:** Craf-T Products
- **metallic copper thread:** Westrim® Crafts
- **24-gage copper wire:** Artistic Wire, Ltd.™
- **deckle decorative scissors:** Family Treasures, Inc.
- **1⁄16" wide circle punch:** Marvy® Uchida
- **copper pen:** Sakura Gelly Roll
- **foam adhesive tape:** Scotch® Brand
- **page designer:** Lisa Garcia-Bergstedt

Rolling waves inspired Arlene to recreate her own with vellum. She started with blue swirls paper for a background, then tore strips of sandstone for the bottom edge. She matted each photo on black then torn white edges. Strips of 1" wide blue and white vellum were torn, then randomly placed with tightly rolled portions wrapped inside the ends of some strips. Arlene used eyelets to attach the overlapping strips to the page. She pulled 4-5 strands of thread through the eyelets along the sides and taped the ends to the back of the page.

- **specialty Paper Pizazz™:** pastel blue vellum, white vellum (by the sheet)
- **patterned Paper Pizazz™:** bright tints blue swirls (*12"x12" Bright Tints*, also by the sheet); sandstone (by the sheet)
- **solid Paper Pizazz™:** white (*Plain Pastels*); black (*Solid Jewel Tones*)
- **10 blue, 6 white eyelets:** Stamp Studio
- **metallic blue thread:** Coats & Clark
- **page designer:** Arlene Peterson

Alyshia
Seaside, Oregon
June 2001

Arlene crafted an antique theme for this lovely page. Floral paper was used for a background, with a ¾"x12" strip of purple vellum glued 1" from the left edge. Working from the top, she attached a 6½"x12" purple vellum rectangle centered on a 9¾"x12" pink/purple stripe with a 1"x12" white strip on the left edge. A sheet of laser lace extends behind the white strip and over purple vellum, with floral paper even with the left edge. For the frame, Arlene cut 5½"x8⅜" rectangles each of floral on purple stripes and paisley then glued their backs together. She cut an "X" through the center (but not cutting to the corners). She glued a photo centered in the opening and matted the whole piece on white. She tightly rolled strips of scrap paper and placed them behind each front section then rolled them back and glued the pieces in place. She stitched the mat edge, catching the rolled pieces. One scallop from each laser lace sheet was cut out and the pieces glued behind the frame as shown.

- **specialty Paper Pizazz™:** 3 sheets of laser lace (by the sheet); pastel purple vellum (*12"x12" Pastel Vellum Papers*, also by the sheet)
- **patterned Paper Pizazz™:** pink/purple stripe, pink/purple floral, floral with purple stripes, purple paisley (*Mixing Light Papers*)
- **solid Paper Pizazz™:** white (*12"x12" Plain Pastels*)
- **metallic silver embroidery thread:** DMC
- **sewing needle**
- **scrap paper**
- **page designer:** Arlene Peterson

Arlene designed a pretty frame with rolled edges for a fun look. She began with blue/green stripes paper for a background. She cut 7"x5½" rectangle each from the diamonds and flowers papers then glued the backs together and cut an "X" in the center (but not cutting to the corners). She placed her photo behind the cutout opening and matted the whole piece on white. She tightly rolled strips of scrap paper and placed them under each rolled back section to form a frame. She glued the folds in place. She punched 10 white daisies and glued one to each frame corner, with a rhinestone in the center. She cut a 12"x2" strip of flowers paper, matted it on white, diamonds then white again. The journal box was printed on white, matted on diamonds then white and glued centered on the strip. Three daisies with rhinestone centers were glued to each end.

- **patterned Paper Pizazz™:** blue/green stripe, white flowers on blue, green/blue diamonds on ivory (*Mixing Light Papers*)
- **solid Paper Pizazz™:** white (*Plain Pastels*)
- **ten ¼" wide pink acrylic rhinestones:** Westrim® Crafts
- **1" wide daisy punch:** Family Treasures, Inc.
- **scrap paper**
- **page designer:** Arlene Peterson

Shrink Plastic

Lisa saw great potential for using shrink plastic to capture a special moment. She began with sepia tile paper for a background, then matted each photo on tan and black. She photocopied the newspaper, reducing it, then foled it and inserted foam tape inside for height. She used the eyeglass pattern on the inside back cover and the manufacturer's instructions to create the shrink plastic glasses, then wrapped wire around the set as shown below. She computer journaled on rectangles of ivory, matted each on black and used foam tape to attach each to the page. It's worth taking a second look!

- **patterned Paper Pizazz™:** 12"x12" sepia tile (by the sheet)
- **solid Paper Pizazz™:** ivory (*Plain Pastels*); tan (*Solid Muted Colors*); black (*Solid Jewel Tones*)
- **shrink plastic:** Shrinky Dinks
- **24-gauge copper wire:** Artistic Wire, Ltd.™
- **E-6000 glue:** Eclectic Products, Inc.
- **foam adhesive tape:** Scotch® Brand
- **page designer:** Lisa Garcia-Bergstedt

wire frame for glasses

Lisa found shrink plastic to make some pearly whites for this adorable page. She used the tooth patterns and the manufacturer's instructions to create two large and one small shrink plastic teeth. She die-cut the letters, matted each on navy, wrapped a strand of yellow fiber around the letters and tooth and glued them to a denim paper background. She placed a 2¾" square of white vellum over the small tooth and stitched it in place with hemp. She looped a strand of blue fiber along the bottom edge of the page. Lisa matted her photo on navy and white. She computer journaled on white and matted it on navy. Lisa used the blue pen for journaling the additional words on the page.

- **specialty Paper Pizazz™:** white vellum (by the sheet)
- **patterned Paper Pizazz™:** denim (by the sheet)
- **solid Paper Pizazz™:** navy (*Solid Muted Colors*); white (*Plain Pastels*)
- **shrink plastic:** Duncan Enterprises
- **schoolhouse letter die-cuts:** Accu/Cut® Systems
- **hemp string, sewing needle:** Westrim® Crafts
- **yellow, blue fibers:** Adornaments™
- **blue pen:** Sakura Gelly Roll
- **foam adhesive tape:** Scotch® Brand
- **page designer:** Lisa Garcia-Bergstedt

Lisa's imagination washed ashore with a lovely collection of seashells and shrink plastic motifs for this stunning page. She transferred the bottle pattern on page 47 and stamped the clock images onto shrink plastic, following the manufacturer's instructions for her motifs. Lisa cut out the lighthouse and shells from one collage paper and used the other for the background. She computer journaled on a 2"x12" strip white vellum, tore the left edge and glued it to the right side of the page. She matted her photo on mauve and dark tan. She journaled on a ¼"x2" strip of white and glued it behind the bottle, then cut out the cork, outlined it in gold and glued it behind the bottle top. Foam tape was used to attach the shells, lighthouse and shrink plastic motifs to the page as shown. Lisa used the black pen for additional journaling.

- **specialty Paper Pizazz™:** white vellum (by the sheet)
- **patterned Paper Pizazz™:** shells & sand collage, lighthouse collage (*Vacation Collage*)
- **solid Paper Pizazz™:** dark tan, mauve (*Solid Muted Colors*); white (*Plain Pastels*)
- **shrink plastic:** Shrinky Dinks
- **clock stamps:** Inkadinkadoo®
- **gold pen:** Sakura Gelly Roll
- **black pens:** Sakura 2mm, 8mm Micron
- **foam adhesive tape:** Scotch® Brand
- **page designer:** Lisa Garcia-Bergstedt

cork

← *shells & sand collage*

lighthouse collage →

Lisa colored shrink plastic to add special highlights for this cheerful page. She trimmed the border paper to the black/white checks, cut out the picture rectangle in the lower right corner, then glued it centered on black with white dots paper. She matted her photo on black. She journaled with the black pen on white, matted it on black, then red, and glued it centered in the cut-out window. She cut eight cherry clusters (see page 1) and a cake slice from shrink plastic, used the colored pencils to add details, then followed the manufacturer's instructions for baking the plastic. The plastic motifs were attached to the page with glue dots™.

- **patterned Paper Pizazz™:** red/black/white border (*Janie Dawson's Special Companions*); black with white dots (by the sheet)
- **solid Paper Pizazz™:** black (*Solid Jewel Tones*); white (*Plain Pastels*); red (*Plain Brights*)
- **shrink plastic:** Shrinky Dinks
- **cake slice, cherries die-cuts:** Accu/Cut® Systems
- **black pen:** Sakura Gelly Roll
- **red, dark green, light green, yellow colored pencils**
- **glue dots:** Glue Dots™ International LLC
- **page designer:** Lisa Garcia-Bergstedt

Accu/Cut® Systems

Stitching

Lisa stitched a quilt to cover this delightful page. Yellow dots made a soft background on which to place a journal box matted on lavender. She used the template to make lavender stripe letters and outlined each in purple. Then she placed each on an ivory square, matted on periwinkle and stitched the squares to the page. Lisa cut forty-two 1" squares from patterned papers, glued them to a 7"x6" piece of ivory and stitched along the edge of each piece. Lisa wrapped ½" wide strips of blue stripes along each edge and sewed them in place. She used the patterns on page 1 to complete the paper doll as shown.

- **patterned Paper Pizazz™:** blue gingham, blue posies, blue stripe, green swirls, green stripe, lavender roses, lavender stripe, lavender swirls, yellow roses, white lilies (*Soft Florals & Patterns*, also by the sheet); yellow dots (*12"x12" Soft Tints*, also by the sheet)
- **solid Paper Pizazz™:** lavender, purple, peach, brown, tan, oatmeal, periwinkle, red-brown (*Solid Muted Colors*); ivory (*Plain Pastels*)
- **lavender, yellow, blue, sage green threads; sewing needle:** Wrights®
- **24-gauge bronze wire:** Artistic Wire, Ltd.™
- **three ⅜" tall wooden spools:** Lara's Crafts
- **pink decorating chalk:** Craf-T Products
- **lettering template:** Frances Meyers®, Inc.
- **⅛" circle, ¼" swirl punches:** Marvy® Uchida
- **metallic purple pen:** Sakura Gelly Roll
- **mini glue dots:** Glue Dots™ International LLC
- **foam adhesive tape, clear tape:** Scotch® Brand
- **page designer:** Lisa Garcia-Bergstedt

Stitching added a golden touch to Shauna's stunning floral collage page. She glued gold micro beads to the centers of the flowers on the collage background paper. A large flower was cut from the companion page and outlined in gold. Shauna stitched thread to the top of the flower, tied a bow with the ribbon and slipped the thread over the bow, so the flower dangled beneath. The photo was matted on gold and centered on white vellum. Shauna tore small squares and rectangles from pastel vellums and placed them behind the photo mat in a mosaic pattern, then stitched the mat to the page. The black pen was used for journaling.

- **specialty Paper Pizazz™:** yellow vellum, light blue vellum, pink vellum, sky blue vellum (*Pastel Vellum Papers*); white vellum (by the sheet); gold (*Metallic Gold*, also by the sheet)
- **patterned Paper Pizazz™:** blossoms on blue collage (*Soft Collage Papers*)
- **metallic gold thread, sewing needle:** Wrights®
- **metallic gold micro beads:** Halcraft USA
- **10" of ½" wide pink sheer ribbon:** C.M. Offray & Son, Inc.
- **gold pen:** Pentel Hybrid Gel Roller
- **black pen:** Sakura Gelly Roll
- **glue dots:** Glue Dots™ International LLC
- **mounting memories glue:** Beacon Adhesives
- **page designer:** Shauna Berglund-Immel

Lisa stitched hearts onto palettes of pink to make this memorable Valentine page. She glued a 1½"x12" strip of pink brushstroke on each side of the pink swirl background paper. Each photo was matted on white, then pink vellum. She cut 8" wire lengths and bent each into a heart following the pattern. Each heart was sewn onto a 2" white square with gold thread. Foam tape was used to attach each heart to a 2¼" square of pink brushstrokes, matted on white, pink vellum and a 3¼" square of pink brushstrokes with torn edges. A circle fastener was inserted in each corner to attach the squares to the page. Lisa tore five 1"-1¼" vellum hearts, then used the heart fasteners to attach one next to each photo and the other three randomly on the page as shown. The black pen was used for journaling.

- **specialty Paper Pizazz™:** pastel pink vellum (*12"x12" Pastel Vellum Papers*, also by the sheet)
- **patterned Paper Pizazz™:** pink brushstroke, pink swirl (*Great Jewel Backgrounds*)
- **solid Paper Pizazz™:** white (*Plain Pastels*)
- **gold thread, sewing needle:** Wrights®
- **⅜" wide heart, ⅛" wide circle fasteners:** Hyglo/AmericanPin
- **24-gauge metallic red wire:** Artistic Wire, Ltd.™
- **metallic pink pen:** Marvy® Uchida
- **black pen:** Sakura 5mm Micron
- **foam adhesive tape:** Scotch® Brand
- **page designer:** Lisa Garcia-Bergstedt

It was "all hands on deck" for LeNae with this patriotic tribute. She cut out letters from navy with stars, matted each on burgundy and stitched them to a tan background. She cut a 12"x7¾" rectangle of red stripe with stars, matted it on ivory and glued it centered on the page. LeNae glued the fabric squares evenly spaced on a 1⅞"x7¾" rectangle of burgundy and matted it on navy. She inserted embroidery thread through each button, knotted the ends and attached one to each fabric square with a glue dot. She matted her photo on ivory, with a torn right edge; then matted it on the left side of a rectangle of navy, with a 2½" border on the right side for journaling and attached a button at each corner.

- **patterned Paper Pizazz™:** red stripe with stars (*Mixing Heritage Papers*); 12"x12" navy with stars (by the sheet)
- **solid Paper Pizazz™:** tan, ivory (*12"x12" Solid Pastel Papers*); navy blue and burgundy (*Solid Jewel Tones*)
- **burgundy, black embroidery thread:** DMC
- **nine ½" wide white buttons**
- **five 1" squares of torn navy/ivory plaid cotton fabric**
- **alphabet template:** Frances Meyer, Inc.® Fat Caps
- **mini glue dots:** Glue Dots™ International LLC
- **clear adhesive tape:** Scotch® Brand
- **black pen:** Zig® Millennium
- **white pen:** Pentel Milky Gel Roller
- **page designer:** LeNae Gerig

Wire

The designs on these metallic patterned papers inspired Shauna to embellish the page with wire and beads. Each photo was matted on red, silver and black then glued to the left side of the silver background sheet. She cut 6⁷/₁₆"x5⁷/₁₆" rectangles each of silver trees on red and silver stars on red; matted each on silver and black then glued them to the right side of the page. She cut one 3"x5" and two 2⅛"x1¼" rectangles of red; matted each on silver and black. The loopy pattern was transferred to the large rectangle, using the silver pen to highlight the design and add dots along the border. She cut a 22" length of wire and used the tree pattern to bend it into shape, threading a bead at the top, then sewing it to the rectangle. The remaining wire was cut in half, with a bead slipped on each. Shauna used the punch to make a hole at each end of both small rectangles, then inserted the wire ends into the holes and taped them at the back to secure. She attached the three rectangles with foam tape to the page as shown.

- **specialty Paper Pizazz™**: silver trees on red, silver stars on red (*Metallic Silver*); 3 sheets of silver (by the sheet)
- **solid Paper Pizazz™**:red, black (*Solid Jewel Tones*)
- **24-gauge silver wire:** Artistic Wire, Ltd.™
- **three ½" wide silver star beads:** Blue Moon Beads/ Elizabeth Ward & Co., Inc.
- **metallic silver thread, sewing needle:** Wrights®
- **¹/₁₆" wide circle punch:** McGill, Inc., Inc.
- **silver pen:** Pentel Hybrid Gel Roller
- **foam adhesive tape, clear tape:** Scotch® Brand
- **tracing paper, transfer paper**
- **wire cutters, pliers**
- **page designer:** Shauna Berglund-Immel

Susan created a spectacular look with wire in this heritage collage. She glued a 3" peach vellum square 1" below the center top edge of the tan nature collage paper. Then she cut 12"x2" strips of ivory and peach vellums and glued them to the page. A 7" square of tan vellum is turned on point and glued to the top of the page. Each photo is matted on white and ivory vellum, with ½"x1" rectangles of white vellum folded onto each corner. For the wire embellishments, Susan cut four 4" lengths, wrapped a 6" length around each and twisted each end into three loops. She tied the ribbon a shoestring bow and wrote the name in white.

- **specialty Paper Pizazz™**: pastel peach vellum, tan vellum (*12"x12" Pastel Vellum Papers*, also by the sheet); ivory vellum, white vellum (by the sheet)
- **patterned Paper Pizazz™:** tan nature collage (*Soft Collage Papers*)
- **24-gauge gold wire:** Artistic Wire, Ltd.™
- **10" of ⅝" wide beige sheer ribbon:** C.M. Offray & Son, Inc.
- **white pen:** Pentel Milky Gel Roller
- **wire cutters, pliers**
- **page designer:** Susan Cobb

fold *fold*

photo corner

Arlene began the page with the diamonds paper for a background. She cut 3³⁄₁₆"x12" and 8¼"x3¼" rectangles of ivory and glued them near the left and bottom edges to form an "L" shape. She cut a 3"x3⅞" and 4⅞"x3" rectangles of floral on green and a 3"x3⅞" and 1½"x3" rectangles of white daisies on blue and glued them as shown. She matted the photo on ivory, floral and ivory papers. Arlene computer journaled on a 2⅝"x3¼" rectangle of ivory and matted it on blue/green stripes. She formed the wire into the loop designs and glued them to the photo mat, journal box and a 1½"x3" rectangle of blue/green stripes as shown. She wrapped metallic thread around the journal box and stripes rectangle then attached them to the page with foam tape.

- **patterned Paper Pizazz™**: blue/green stripe, green/blue diamonds on ivory, white daisies on blue, floral on green (*Mixing Light Papers*)
- **solid Paper Pizazz™**: ivory (*Plain Pastels*)
- **24-gauge metallic aqua wire**: Artistic Wire, Ltd.™
- **metallic aqua thread**: Coats & Clark
- **foam adhesive tape**: Scotch® Brand
- **page designer**: Arlene Peterson

Lisa created wire embellishments to adorn this precious page. She used coordinating patterned and vellum papers for a soft look. The pink floral bordered paper was the background. She cut two 6"x4" rectangles from the white dots and pink swirl/leaf vellums, tearing one long side of each rectangle. The rectangles were overlapped, with the torn edges toward the center of the page. Lisa tore a 2½"x5¾" rectangle from each of two patterned vellums and used pink chalk along the edges; then placed them slightly overlapping in a vertical direction on the page. The photo was matted on pink and white then glued centered on the page. Lisa inserted silver eyelets near the photo; then inserted a 10" wire through the eyelets, twirling the ends as shown. A white eyelet was inserted into each corner of the page. Lisa used the remaining wire to form four five-loop daisies, inserted one into each eyelet and used tape to adhere it to the page back. She journaled with the pink pen on 1" wide strips of white vellum.

- **specialty Paper Pizazz™**: pink floral bordered paper, pink swirl/leaf vellum, white dotted vellum (*Mixing Papers & Vellum*); white vellum (by the sheet)
- **solid Paper Pizazz™**: white, pink (*Solid Muted Colors*)
- **4 silver, 4 white eyelets**: Stamp Studio
- **pink decorating chalk**: Craf-T Products
- **24-gauge metallic burgundy wire**: Artistic Wire, Ltd.™
- **metallic pink pen**: Marvy® Uchida
- **page designer**: Lisa Garcia-Bergstedt

Wire

Hailey And Grandma
November 2001

Lisa served a full course of fun with this spectacular page. She began with navy stars for a background. She matted one photo on red and blue and reversed the colors for her second photo. She used the patterns on the inside back cover to cut the apron as shown and stitched the pockets with white pen. She cut out the spatula from foil, then cut two ¼"x2" strips, placing one on the wooden handle top and wrapping the other to secure it. She used the patterns below to form the grill and skewers from wire and beads as shown. She inserted eyelets in the apron and threaded hemp as shown. She cut the letters from blue and matted each on red.

- **patterned Paper Pizazz™:** navy stars on ivory, navy stars on stripes (*Mixing Heritage Papers*)
- **solid Paper Pizazz™:** navy, red (*Solid Jewel Tones*); white (*Plain Pastels*)
- **22-gauge black, gray wire:** Artistic Wire, Ltd.™
- **jewel mix matte beads:** Blue Moon Beads/Elizabeth Ward & Co., Inc.
- **4 silver eyelets:** Stamp Studio
- **ArtEmboss™ aluminum foil:** American Art Clay Co., Inc.
- **½"x6" strip of balsa wood**
- **hemp string:** Westrim® Crafts
- **⅛" wide silver fastener:** Hyglo/AmericanPin
- **schoolhouse letter die-cuts:** Accu/Cut® Systems
- **black pen:** Sakura 5mm Micron
- **white pen:** Pentel Milky Gel Roller
- **wire cutters, pliers**
- **foam adhesive tape:** Scotch® Brand
- **tracing paper, transfer paper**
- **page designer:** Lisa Garcia-Bergstedt

Arlene curled wire for a whimsical addition to this sweetheart page. She began with the hearts/words on pink background. A 7¼"x10¾" rectangle of pink/yellow plaid was matted on ivory and glued to the right side of the page. Arlene matted two photos on a 6⅛"x8⅛" rectangle of ivory, then glued it to the plaid mat as shown. She used the patterns to make two quilted hearts and one whole heart from the patterned papers then matted each on ivory, trimming the edges with the decorative scissors. She stitched the pieces together as shown. Three faces were cut from ivory and glued behind the hearts. Arlene cut wire into 15 pieces, then used the needle to curl each one. She used tape to attach five wire pieces to each heart face as shown. The black pen was used to draw eyes.

- **patterned Paper Pizazz™:** hearts/words on pink, pink/yellow plaid, pink flowers on yellow, pink squares on ivory, pink/yellow stripe (*Mixing Light Papers*)
- **solid Paper Pizazz™:** 2 sheets of ivory (*Plain Pastels*)
- **24-gauge copper wire:** Artistic Wire, Ltd.™
- **pink decorating chalk:** Craf-T Products
- **3" wide heart die-cut:** Accu/Cut® Systems
- **bright pink embroidery thread:** DMC
- **sewing needle**
- **scallop decorative scissors:** Fiskars®
- **clear adhesive tape:** Scotch® Brand
- **black pen:** Sakura 5mm Micron
- **page designer:** Arlene Peterson

Each year everyone who lives on Millers Road gathers for the Annual 4ᵗʰ of July BBQ. It is always good fun and great memories for everyone. We start with the BBQ and then we move on to games and finally the fireworks. Each year it is fun to see who is new to the neighborhood and to gather with those who have shared in this event for the past 10 years.

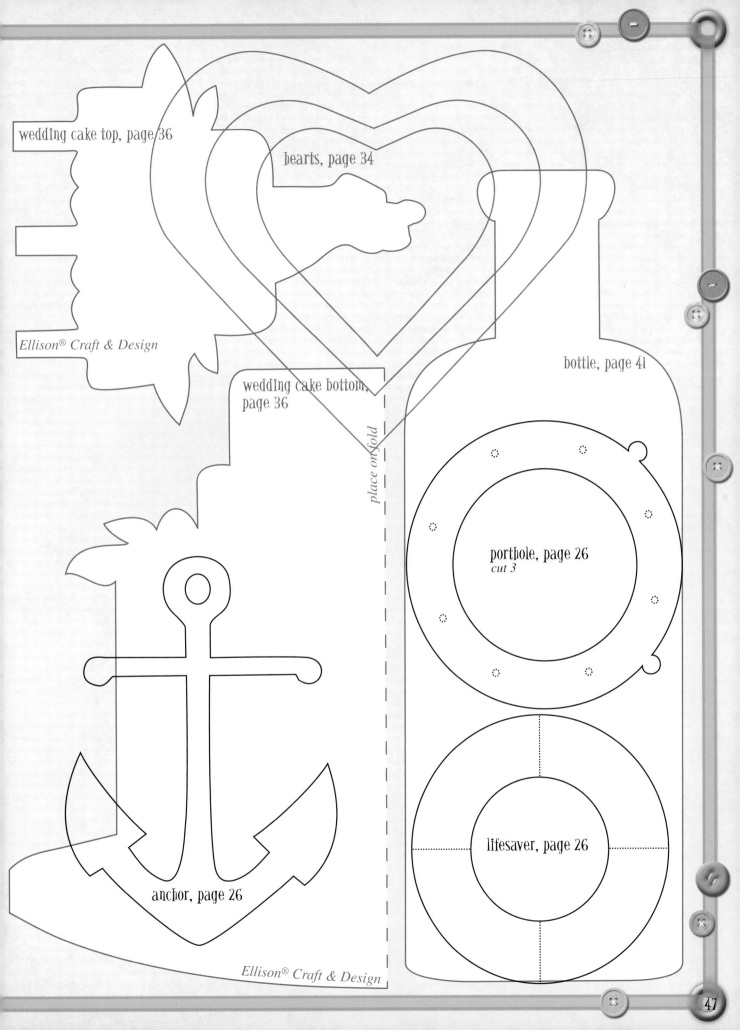

wedding cake top, page 36

hearts, page 34

Ellison® Craft & Design

bottle, page 41

wedding cake bottom,
page 36

place on fold

porthole, page 26
cut 3

anchor, page 26

lifesaver, page 26

Ellison® Craft & Design

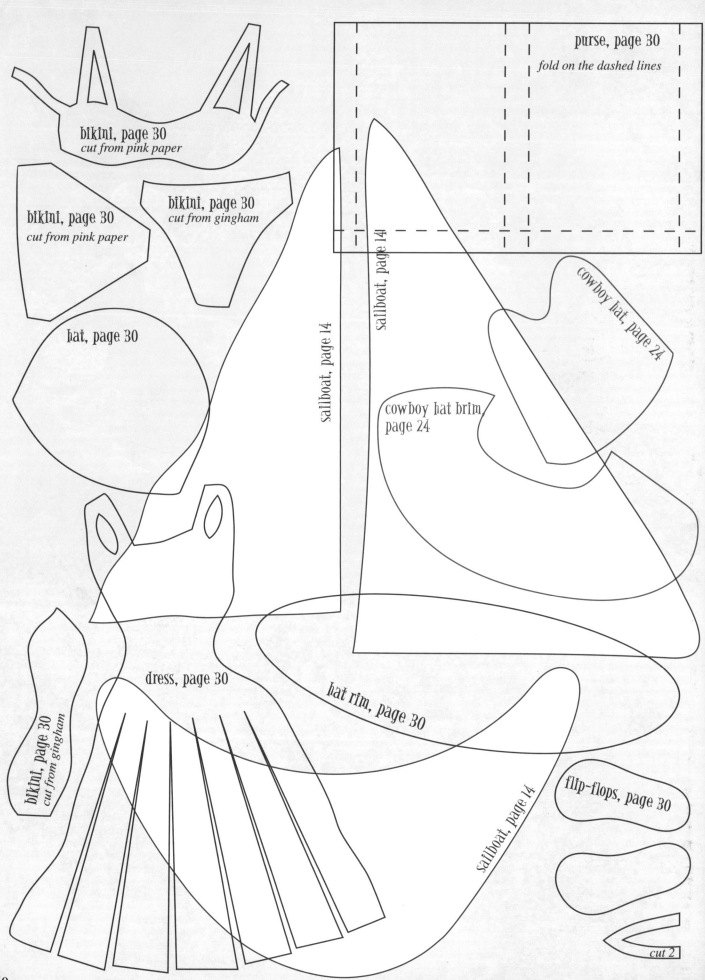

bikini, page 30
cut from pink paper

bikini, page 30
cut from pink paper

bikini, page 30
cut from gingham

purse, page 30
fold on the dashed lines

hat, page 30

sailboat, page 14

sailboat, page 14

cowboy hat, page 24

cowboy hat brim, page 24

dress, page 30

bikini, page 30
cut from gingham

hat rim, page 30

sailboat, page 14

flip-flops, page 30

cut 2